Delights of the Jewish Kitchen
Cakes, Cookies and Pastries

TZIPPORA KREIZMAN

Delights of the Jewish Kitchen
Cakes, Cookies and Pastries

 KOSHER

Kreizman Publications
Jerusalem 5764

First published in Hebrew as *Nichochot HaMa'afeh*
by Kreizman Publications (1993)

English translation: Fern Zekbach

Graphic Design: Harvey Klineman
Illustrations: Yoni Gerstein
Photographs: Nelly Sheffer Studio
Production and Styling of Photographs: Nurit Barnitzky
Typesetting: Hannah Hartman
Accessories appearing in photographs
courtesy of Canaan; Bordo; and Rosenthal.

Cover Photo: Special Filled Sponge Cake, page 90

ISBN 1-58330-514-9

First published 2004

KREIZMAN PUBLICATIONS
22 Sorotzkin Street
Jerusalem, Israel
Tel.: (2) 537-1450 / 052-483-939

Distributed by:

FELDHEIM PUBLISHERS
POB 43163 / Jerusalem, Israel

208 Airport Executive Park
Nanuet, NY 10954

www.feldheim.com

10 9 8 7 6 5 4 3 2 1

Printed in Israel

TZIPPORA KREIZMAN
of blessed memory

It is most fitting to open this wonderful book with a few words about the author, Tzippora Kreizman, *a"h*, who was a very special person. A woman of valor imbued with pure Jewish faith and blessed with many talents and strengths, she skillfully wove the traditions and customs of the Jewish people into practical daily life. She baked and cooked, preparing tasty dishes with a prayer of thanksgiving for her ability to enhance the Sabbath and Holiday table, as well as everyday cuisine, with good taste and beauty.

In this book, great effort was made by the author to ensure that the text would be clearly phrased and the instructions easy to follow. The recipes are precise, and call for ingredients commonly on hand and easy on the pocketbook. The author adapted the recipes so that they would be appropriate both for women taking their first steps in the kitchen as well as those who have long been at home there.

Tzippora Kreizman, *a"h*, was a kind and compassionate woman. She attended to every detail in everything she did, and with a warm and loving heart she joyously helped the many people who turned to her for advice both in the kitchen and out of it.

May the wonderful aromas of baking that arise from this book become a "pleasing fragrance" together with Tzippora Kreizman's virtues and merits. May she be a *melitzat yosher*, a Heavenly advocate, for us from Above.

Contents

From the Author's Preface
to the Hebrew Edition

"Lekach un branfen," cake and *schnaps*, is a deeply entrenched, widespread Jewish custom, accompanying special occasions from the day of birth to the end of life — a faithful companion.

Each newborn baby is greeted with great excitement, and along with the *"mazal tov"* and handshakes comes a piece of cake and a drink. Baked goods continue to be part of every significant occasion, at the *shalom zachor* for a son and at the *kiddush* celebrating the arrival of a daughter.

And what loftier event do we have than the bris? The cry of the new baby boy who has just joined the Jewish people mixes with the tears of joy and good wishes of those in attendance, who then recite a blessing over cake and drink.

When the little boy has become a toddler and celebrates his third birthday, he moves on to another stage in his Jewish identity. His hair is cut, and he now has *payos* and a *kippah.* All present at the celebration will partake of cake and drink.

He is so proud at his *"Chumash* party." He recites his first *d'var Torah*, at the age of five, surrounded by family and friends wishing him well and making a blessing on cake and drink to celebrate the occasion.

Thus childhood goes by, and the bar mitzvah arrives. At thirteen the boy is no longer a happy-go-lucky child, but an adult Jew who takes upon himself the yoke of the commandments. The donning of *tefillin* and a special festive meal, the *se'udas mitzvah*, takes place, including a rich assortment of cakes and beverages.

The young man diligently continues, swimming in the sea of Torah study, becoming more serious and mature. The time comes to settle down. With joy and thanksgiving he leaves his parents' home and establishes his own. The clinking of glasses and a piece of cake are an essential part of the *vort*, when the first steps are taken in forging the link between the engaged *chosson* and *kallah*.

A *se'udas mitzvah* and trays laden with cakes are served at the writing of the *tenaim*, the engagement party. Then comes the wedding day and its blessings, followed by dancing and joyousness, along with a *se'udas mitzvah* and a wealth of cakes.

A new house, a new family. The young girl of yesterday has now become a wife. She gains expertise in cooking and baking: *challos*, cakes, and cookies for Shabbos and holidays the whole year through. She will bake for her own family as well as for the celebrations of others.

It is not that the shelves of commercial bakeries do not offer a wonderful choice of baked goods! It is that home-baked goods contain that special ingredient which makes them irreplaceable: love and joy in honor of the mitzvah.

Cakes and blessings. Cakes and mitzvos. Rich, varied baking that accompanies the passing of the weeks and years. And when a Jew's time has come and he is called to the World on High, his day of departure will be commemorated every year with the study of *mishnayos* in his honor, and all the participants will partake of the refreshments and pronounce a blessing over cake and drink.

With heartfelt wishes for productive, satisfying baking.

Tzippora Kreizman
Tevet, 5753

Introduction

Each recipe in this book comes with a short introduction. The clear and precise instructions will help young bakers just starting out as well as those with years of experience. A note accompanies each recipe telling you if the item freezes well or not.

The recipes have been divided into the following groups:

Nuts — From light tortes rich in nuts to special layer cakes. Baking with nuts is part of Simchas Torah, Purim, and private celebrations and festivities.

Cheese — A large, impressive selection of different types of baked goods made with cheese. Cheese cakes made with flaky pastry, yeast dough, puff pastry, folded dough, or a sponge-cake base. Cheese cakes are good on any Shabbos and especially on Shavuos — when they are richly decorated or feature wonderful combinations.

Honey — Wonderfully aromatic, browned cakes and cookies. Honey cakes are part of Rosh Hashanah, Purim, Shavuos, or any *simchah* where *"Lekach un branfen"* (cake and *shnaps*) are offered.

Dobos — Beautiful, festive slices, with a tasty, delicate filling between the layers. Having a rich chocolate frosting, *pareve* or dairy, these cakes are great at *simchas.*

Tortes — Sponge cakes, light and airy, that match any occasion. They can be enriched, decorated, or frosted.

Cake Rolls — Beautiful cake rolls made from thin sheets of sponge cake rolled around great fillings. Cake rolls are elegant with their variety of fruit or icing fillings that can accompany any festive event or *simchah.*

Crescents — A striking selection of crescent-shaped cookies made from yeast dough, folded dough, flaky pastry, or puff pastry. They can be made with a variety of fillings, from the simplest — good on any Shabbos — to richest — baked for holidays and *simchas.*

Strudels — Cakes rolled from very thin dough with a variety of wonderful fillings. Strudels can be matched to an occasion or holiday by their fillings.

A Miscellany — Cakes baked as individual serving portions. These include cream puffs, blintz-type baked goods, cream-filled minicakes, and so on — all very tasty and attractive.

Cakes with Fruit — A variety of suggestions for using fruits in season. Fruits can be used with flaky pastry or sponge cake, simple or adorned with whipped cream, jellied desserts, and so on. Fruit cakes are rich and special.

Yeast Cakes — Ever-popular yeast cakes are found on the cake tray every Shabbos and holiday. Fresh, cold, or folded yeast dough — with a variety of fillings and suggestions for baking and serving.

Layer Cakes — Many beautiful, scrumptious cakes are in this section; they are made in stages. The cakes consist of different layers — and almost all of them covered with rich frostings or glazes. Every one of these is good for festive events.

Cookies — A rich variety of different types of cookies, large tasty batches, easy to make. Here are cookies ranging from everyday ones to festive, rich ones for holidays and special occasions.

Delights of the Jewish Kitchen
Cakes, Cookies and Pastries

NUT CAKES, particularly almond cakes, conjure up the special aura of cake baking. The ingredients used in them are not inexpensive, but each slice is first-class and special. The combination of ground walnuts and almonds turn a plain torte into a festive, delicate cake. A filling of chopped nuts, made richer with the addition of chocolate, changes a cake with a good flaky dough into one for special occasions. Nuts and almonds go well with any kind of dough and are used in piecrusts, yeast doughs, phyllo pastries, and sponge cakes. Rich nut cakes always enhance family celebrations and holidays.

Nut Cakes

Nut and Mousse Cake

More of a delectable dessert than a regular cake. The cake has three layers: the first and third, a thin layer enriched with bits of nuts; the middle, a delicate mousse filling. A great cake to send to others on festive occasions. You can make this cake dairy or nondairy. Freezes well.

BATTER

1 cup hazelnuts, coarsely chopped
¾ cup salted margarine
½ cup sugar
¾ cup self-rising flour

FILLING

4 ounces bittersweet chocolate
2 tablespoons water
2 tablespoons sugar
3 eggs, separated
250 ml (1 cup) whipping cream OR nondairy substitute
2 teaspoons vanilla

Preparing the batter: Combine hazelnuts, margarine, sugar, and flour. Separate batter into two equal parts. Line a 10-inch round baking pan with aluminum foil; lightly grease the foil. Spread one-half of the batter into pan, not quite reaching the edges (cake will spread during baking). Bake this layer in a preheated oven at 350°F (180°C) for 15 minutes. Remove from oven. Let cool a bit. Using the foil, carefully transfer the baked layer to a serving plate.

☞ Bake the second half of the batter in the same way. Keep it in the baking pan until you assemble the cake.

Preparing the filling: Break chocolate into pieces. Place in a saucepan with the water, place over a pan with boiling water and stir constantly, until the chocolate melts. Pour into a bowl, add the egg yolks, and mix thoroughly.

☞ In a separate bowl, beat egg whites, gradually adding sugar, until peaks are firm. Fold beaten egg whites into the chocolate mixture.

☞ Whip the dairy or nondairy whipping cream, while adding the vanilla. Gently fold whipped cream into the chocolate mixture.

Assembling the cake: Gently spread the whipped cream over the first layer. Carefully set the second baked layer over the filling, and peel off the aluminum foil. Refrigerate until serving. Cut into wedges and serve. For easier serving, the cake may be partially frozen before cutting.

Nut and Chocolate Cake

An excellent layer cake — a bottom white cake layer rich with nuts and a dark upper covering of whipped chocolate. This cake is attractive, tasty, and fit for serving on festive occasions. Freezes well.

WHITE CAKE

¾ cup salted margarine

¾ cup sugar

1 egg

1 yolk

1½ cups hazelnuts, finely chopped

1½ cups self-rising flour

DARK FROSTING

3 heaping tablespoons jam

8 ounces baking chocolate, broken into pieces

¾ cup unsalted margarine, cut into cubes

5 egg yolks

6 egg whites

¾ cup sugar

2 tablespoons flour — optional

Preparing the white layer: In a bowl, mix margarine and sugar. Stir in egg, yolk, nuts, and flour. Lightly grease a 9x11-inch baking pan. Line it with the dough, pressing evenly. Bake in a preheated oven at 350°F (180°C) for about 20 minutes. Remove the pan from the oven, and spread jam over cake.

Preparing the dark layer: Put chocolate pieces and margarine cubes into a small pan. Place over low heat. Melt together, stirring constantly with a wooden spoon. Remove from heat, and gently stir in the egg yolks, mixing thoroughly.

In a separate bowl, while gradually adding the sugar, beat the egg whites until stiff peaks form. Gently fold the chocolate mixture into beaten egg whites. (Fold in flour — optional.)

Pour the chocolate/egg white mixture over the jam. Return pan to oven. Lower heat to 325°F (170°C), and bake 40 minutes. Turn off oven, and let cake remain in it for about 20 minutes.

NUT CAKES

Elegant Nut Cake [picture on page 22]

Looking for a large, beautiful, elegant cake? — here it is! The cake's five layers take some effort, but it is worth it. The base layer is a light sponge cake, covered with frosting. Next comes a layer of rich nut cake, also frosted. Topping all is a smooth chocolate layer. Serve cut into small squares. This cake freezes well.

NUT CAKE (BAKED FIRST)

12 eggs, separated

2½ cups sugar

2 teaspoons vanilla

1 cup baking chocolate, coarsely grated

1½ cups nuts, finely chopped

¼ cup liqueur

4 tablespoons self-rising flour

SPONGE CAKE BASE

5 eggs, separated

¾ cup sugar

¾ cup self-rising flour

¼ cup cocoa

COCOA FROSTING

2 eggs

1 cup unsalted margarine

1 cup confectioner's sugar

2 tablespoons cocoa

1 tablespoon instant coffee powder

2 tablespoons rum or wine

CHOCOLATE GLAZE

5 ounces bittersweet chocolate, broken into pieces

2 tablespoons water

½ cup unsalted margarine

Note: First bake the nut cake, and remove it from the baking pan. Then in the same pan bake the sponge cake that will be the bottom layer for the whole assembly.

Preparing the nut cake: Place the egg yolks into a large bowl. Beat lightly with ½ cup of the sugar and the vanilla. Add, while stirring, chocolate, nuts, and liqueur. In a separate bowl, beat the egg whites until peaks are firm, gradually adding the remaining sugar. Stir beaten egg whites into yolk mixture. Carefully fold the flour into the mixture.

Line 15x10-inch pan with baking parchment. Pour batter into pan. Bake in a preheated oven at 350°F (180°C) for about 45 minutes. Insert toothpick to check if done. Remove the cake from the tin and set it on a tray.

Preparing the sponge cake: In a bowl, beat egg whites until peaks are firm, while gradually adding the sugar. Gently stir beaten egg whites into yolk mixture. Sift cocoa powder into the flour. Stirring gently, add flour mixture to beaten whites. Line the baking pan with baking parchment. Pour batter into pan. Bake at 350°F (180°C) for 15 minutes. Insert toothpick to check if done. Remove from oven when toothpick comes out clean.

Preparing the frosting: In the order listed, put the ingredients into a food processor or blender. Mix all until smooth and velvety. For best results, refrigerate until firm.

Assembling the cake: Refrigerate the base layer for a short time. Then spread half the frosting on it. Place the baked nut cake over the frosting. Spread the remaining frosting over it. Freeze for one hour. When the top frosting is frozen, you will be able to spread the chocolate glaze without it sinking into the cocoa frosting.

Preparing the chocolate glaze: Place bittersweet chocolate and water into the top of a double boiler and melt over boiling water. When the chocolate is soft, mix it with the margarine. Spread chocolate over the frozen cake with a broad, flat knife, spreading to a smooth, uniform finish. When ready, the cake can be returned to the freezer to be used at a later date or to the refrigerator until served.

Nut Dzerbo

A gorgeous Hungarian cake, wonderful for festive occasions. This cake has three flaky layers and a rich nut filling and is topped with a chocolate glaze. This cake freezes well.

DOUGH

1 packet dry yeast

scant ⅓ cup orange juice or water

3 cups flour

1¼ cups salted margarine

2 eggs

3 tablespoons sugar

1 tablespoon lemon juice

FILLING

4 tablespoons high-quality jam

3 cups nuts, finely chopped

1 cup sugar

2 tablespoons grated lemon rind

CHOCOLATE GLAZE

3 tablespoons sugar

2 tablespoons cocoa powder

1 tablespoon instant coffee powder

3 tablespoons water

¼ cup unsalted margarine

Preparing the dough: Soften yeast in the liquid. Sift flour into a bowl. Make a well in the middle of the flour, and pour yeast mixture into it. Add other ingredients, and knead into a pliable dough, easy to roll out. (You may have to adjust the amount of liquid, depending on the stiffness of the dough.) Shape into a ball, cover, and refrigerate for one hour. Flour a work surface. Remove dough from refrigerator, and divide into three equal portions.

Lightly grease a 15x10-inch baking pan. Roll out a portion of the dough to the size of the pan, and place dough into pan.

Preparing the filling: In a bowl, mix nuts, sugar, and grated lemon rind. Spread two tablespoons of fine jam evenly over the dough. Sprinkle half the nut filling over the jam. Roll out the second portion of dough. Cover the filling with dough. Spread the remaining jam over it. Sprinkle the remainder of the nut filling over the jam. Roll out the third portion of dough to a size a bit larger than the baking pan — it will shrink during baking. Place it on top of the cake. Prick well with fork to allow steam to escape during baking.

☙ Bake the cake in a preheated oven at 350°F (180°C) for about 45 minutes until lightly browned.

Preparing the glaze: In a small saucepan, put sugar, cocoa, coffee, and water. Cook over a medium flame, stirring constantly with a wooden spoon until all ingredients have melted into a chocolate syrup.

☙ Remove pan from heat. Add margarine to the syrup, and stir until glaze is smooth. Pour the glaze over the cake and spread with a spatula.

☙ To serve — cut the cake into small, delicate squares.

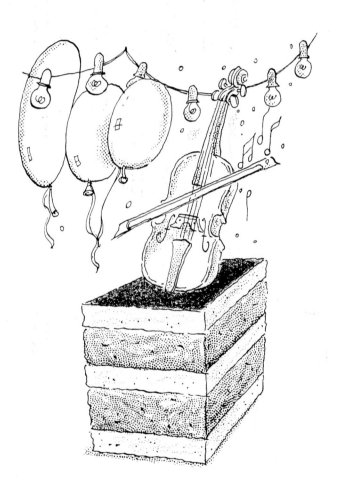

NUT CAKES

Puff Pastry Layered Nut Torte

An elegant, rich taste treat. This cake has an upper and a lower layer made from puff pastry. In between comes a speckled torte enriched with nuts. Sandwiched between the flaky layers and the torte is a layer of chocolate frosting. As a variation, you can use a chocolate torte in place of the nut. A dusting of confectioner's sugar tops the cake. A specialty that goes a long way on happy occasions. This cake freezes well.

DOUGH
1 pound, 10 ounces puff pastry

NUT TORTE
9 eggs, separated
1½ cups sugar
2 tablespoons oil
¼ cup wine
1 teaspoon grated lemon rind
1 cup ground nuts
1 cup of self-rising flour

CHOCOLATE TORTE
9 eggs, separated
1½ cups sugar
2 tablespoons oil
1 teaspoon vanilla extract
3½ teaspoons vanilla sugar
¼ cup wine
½ cup cocoa powder
2 tablespoons ground nuts — optional
1 cup self-rising flour OR
    1 cup regular flour + 1 level teaspoon baking powder

CHOCOLATE FROSTING
8 ounces baking chocolate, broken into pieces
1 tablespoon instant coffee powder
¾ cup sugar
¼ cup water
2 cups unsalted margarine, cut into cubes
2 eggs

DECORATION

confectioner's sugar

Preparing the dough: Divide dough into two parts. Lightly flour a work surface. Roll each part out until a bit larger than a 15x10-inch baking pan. Lightly flour the outside of the baking pan, and cover it with the sheet of dough. Prick thoroughly with a fork.

♟ Heat the oven to 450°F (220°C). Bake each sheet of dough for 12 minutes, until nicely puffed. Carefully remove baked pastry from the pan and put on a tray.

Preparing the nut torte: In a bowl, beat yolks with ½ cup of sugar. Mix in oil, wine, and lemon. While gradually adding the remaining sugar, beat the whites until peaks are stiff. Carefully mix in the nuts. Gently fold yolk mixture into beaten egg whites. Fold flour into egg mixture, using broad strokes.

♟ Line the baking pan with baking parchment. Pour batter into it, and smooth evenly with a spatula.

♟ Bake in a preheated oven at 350°F (180°C) for about 50 minutes. Insert a toothpick to check if done. It is ready when toothpick comes out clean. Remove cake from pan, and place on a tray.

Preparing the chocolate torte: Mixing method is identical to the nut torte. You may stir the cocoa into the yolk mixture at the beginning of the process. Fold in beaten egg whites, nuts — for a richer cake — and, last, the flour.

Preparing the frosting: Put pieces of chocolate, instant coffee powder, sugar, and water into a pan. Stirring constantly with a wooden spoon, cook over a medium flame until a syrup is formed. Pour the syrup into a mixer bowl or food processor, add cubed margarine and eggs. Mix into a smooth, velvety frosting. For best results, refrigerate frosting for an hour to become firm.

Assembling the cake: Place one of the baked puff pastry layers on a serving tray. Spread half the frosting over it.

♟ Carefully place the torte over the frosting, with the aluminum foil on top. Carefully peel off foil. Spread the remaining frosting over the torte. Place the second puff pastry layer over the frosting. Sprinkle confectioner's sugar over the top.

Note: If you would like cake slices that are less high, reduce the torte recipe by one-third. The lovely baked torte will be of normal height.

Variations: For variety, you can use other frostings. Instead of chocolate, try mocha, lemon, or vanilla; for an interesting change, use nondairy whip. Beat one container of nondairy whip until firm while gradually adding 2 tablespoons sugar. Continue to beat while adding one package of vanilla instant pudding to obtain a delicately flavored frosting.

NUT CAKES

Elegant Nut Sandwich Cake

Cut small slices of this sumptuous cake. The nut cake is baked in one large, thin layer. After baking it is cut in two and arranged like a sandwich cake, with a special chocolate filling in the middle. To make it even richer, you can drizzle a chocolate glaze on top (see Almond-Base Torte, page 16). This cake can be made as an elegant cake roll, decorated with chopped nuts or other similar toppings. This cake freezes well.

CAKE

5 egg whites

1 cup sugar

2 tablespoons cocoa powder, sifted

2 tablespoons flour

2 tablespoons toasted breadcrumbs

1 cup nuts, finely chopped

FILLING

¾ cup unsalted margarine

3 tablespoons cognac

1 teaspoon vanilla

4 ounces chocolate, broken into bits

5 egg yolks

Preparing the cake: Put the egg whites into a bowl; gradually adding the sugar, beat until stiff peaks form. Gently fold in cocoa, flour, breadcrumbs, and nuts into the beaten egg whites, continuing until all ingredients are well blended.

☞ Preheat oven to 350°F (180°C).

☞ Line a 15x10-inch baking pan with baking parchment. Pour the batter into the pan, gently smoothing the top with a spatula. Bake 10 to 15 minutes. Check for readiness by inserting a toothpick. If it comes out clean, cake is ready. Let cake cool on tabletop. Divide it into two equal parts.

Preparing the filling: Put egg yolks into a bowl. Place margarine, cognac, vanilla, and chocolate into a saucepan. Stirring constantly, melt over a medium flame. When the syrup is ready, stir a few drops of the mixture into egg yolks. Mix well and, while stirring, pour yolks into syrup. (*Note:* no sugar is necessary.)

☞ Pour chocolate mixture into bowl of a food processor. Process for 20 minutes until filling is light, clear, and uniform.

Assembling the cake: Line a large tray with baking parchment whose edges can be folded high. Place the first layer of the nut cake on the tray. Spread the filling on it. It is recommended to freeze the cake at this stage for 20 minutes to harden the filling a bit. Then place the second layer over the filling. If you wish, drizzle a cooked chocolate glaze over the cake.

Variations:

1) You can divide the filling into two parts. Use one half as filling between layers, the other as frosting over the top layer. If you are using a chocolate glaze, freeze the cake before spreading the glaze. The contrast between light and dark brown make the cake very attractive.

2) Instead of cutting cake in two, make a cake roll out of it. Immediately upon removing the cake from the oven, turn it out onto a dishtowel sprinkled liberally with confectioner's sugar or flour. Roll the cake up with the towel, let it rest for a few minutes, then unroll. Spread all or half the chocolate filling on it, roll the cake up jelly-roll fashion. If you reserved half the frosting, spread it over the cake roll. For best results, partially freeze before cutting.

NUT CAKES

Layered Nut and Mousse Cake

A tasty, rich, attractive cake, more of a confection and a dessert than a hearty cake. The base is a delicate crumb layer, followed by a layer of feathery mousse and a layer of decorated whipped cream. The whipped layer can be dairy or nondairy. This cake stands out when sent as mishlo'ach manot on Purim, as a gift on a festive occasion, and so on.

BASE LAYER

6 eggs, separated

1 cup sugar

6 ounces bittersweet chocolate, cut into small pieces

⅓ cup brandy

3 tablespoons water

1 cup salted margarine (or butter)

4 level tablespoons cake or bread crumbs

1 cup ground nuts

MOUSSE WHIP

2–3 tablespoons jam

1 cup whipping cream or nondairy substitute

sugar: for sweetened cream or substitute — 1 heaping tablespoon

for unsweetened cream or substitute — ½ cup

1 teaspoon instant coffee powder OR

2 tablespoons vanilla instant pudding — optional

TOPPING

Chocolate glaze (Almond-Base Torte, page 16) or chocolate sprinkles nut halves, sugared cherries

Preparing the cake: Put egg whites into a bowl. Beat while gradually adding ½ cup sugar until the peaks are firm.

☙ Put chocolate pieces into a saucepan. Add brandy and water. Melt over a low flame, stirring constantly. Add margarine (or butter), and continue to stir until mixture is smooth. Pour the hot syrup, while stirring slowly, into the bowl with the yolks. Fold beaten egg whites into chocolate mixture.

☙ Divide chocolate mixture into two. Refrigerate one half for 3–4 hours to become firm (or place in freezer for shorter time). To the remaining half, add the crumbs and the nuts, stirring gently.

☞ Lightly grease an 11-inch round baking pan. Preferably use an attractive heat-resistant pan. Turn the crumb mixture into the pan. Preheat the oven to 350°F (180°C), and bake the cake for 25 minutes. Check to see if cake is ready by inserting a toothpick. If it comes out clean, the cake is done. Remove baked cake from the oven and cool.

Assembling the cake: Spread jam on the baked base layer. On top of the jam, gently spread the refrigerated portion of the mousse. Refrigerate the cake.

☞ Pour the whipping cream or nondairy whip into a bowl. Beat it while adding the amount of sugar listed. We recommend using instant coffee powder or vanilla pudding for added interest. Remove cake from refrigerator, and carefully spread the whip over the mousse layer. Decorate the cake as your imagination dictates or for that special occasion. For example, you can toss chocolate sprinkles on top, or draw asymmetrical lines in the whip with a fork. Finish by adding nut halves and sugared cherries alternately around the top.

Variation: Before adding the instant coffee powder to the whip, set aside ½ cup of the firm whip and put it into a decorator's tube. Pipe rosettes on the mocha whip. Put a cherry or chocolate coffee bean in the center of each rosette.

☞ Store cake in freezer until one hour before serving.

Almond-Base Torte

A tasty cake assembled in layers, easy to prepare. The crispy base is covered with a thin layer of jam. On top of that comes a delicate almond mixture. The cake's height comes from a torte layer set atop the almond layer. You can make the cake even richer by adding a chocolate glaze. Freezes well.

DOUGH

2 cups flour

2 teaspoons baking powder

1 cup salted margarine, cut into 8 cubes

scant ½ cup sugar

3 egg yolks

grated rind of a lemon

scant ⅓ cup orange juice or water

FILLING

3 tablespoons jam

120 grams almonds, hazelnuts, or peanuts, ground

scant ½ cup sugar

¼ cup cake crumbs

1 egg white

TORTE

5 eggs, separated

1¼ cups sugar

1 tablespoon cognac

1 tablespoon lemon rind, finely ground

⅓ cup oil

1¼ cups flour

2 teaspoons baking powder

CHOCOLATE GLAZE — OPTIONAL

2 tablespoons powdered cocoa

½ cup sugar

scant ⅓ cup wine

¼ cup unsalted margarine

1 egg yolk

Preparing the dough: Sift flour and baking power; add margarine. Add sugar, egg yolks, lemon, and juice. Work into a spongy, soft dough; you may have to adjust the liquids. Lightly grease a 9x13-inch baking pan, and line the pan with the dough. Bake in a preheated oven at 350°F (180°C) for about 10 minutes. Remove the pan from the oven (the dough will be half-baked), and spread the jam evenly over the dough.

Preparing the filling: In a bowl, stir together the almonds, sugar, crumbs, and egg white. Gently spread the mixture over the jam layer.

Preparing the torte: Put egg yolks into a bowl, and beat lightly with ¼ cup sugar. Stir in cognac, lemon, and oil. In a separate bowl, while gradually adding the remaining sugar, beat the egg whites until peaks are firm. Fold beaten egg whites into the yolk mixture. Combine flour and baking powder, and fold into the egg mixture. Pour batter over filling. Return cake pan to the oven, and bake for 40 minutes. (To check if ready, insert a toothpick. If it comes out dry, cake is ready.)

Preparing the chocolate glaze: The cake may be served without the glaze. If you do wish to add it, put cocoa, sugar, and liquids into a small saucepan. Stir with a wooden spoon over a medium flame until the mixture becomes syrupy. Turn off the fire. Melt the margarine by stirring it in the warm syrup. Add egg yolk, and stir until syrup is smooth and delicate. Drizzle the syrup asymmetrically over the cake.

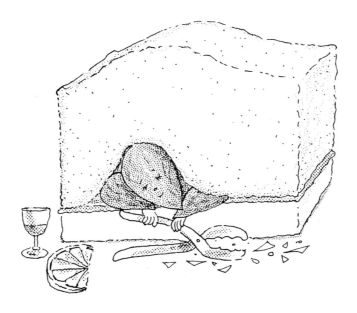

Nut Slices

A small, pretty, delicate cake. The crispy base is covered with jam. On top of it comes a layer of chopped nuts and chocolate, all crowned with white meringue. As a variation, you can use coconut and chocolate in place of the nuts. Freezes well.

DOUGH
¾ cup salted margarine, at room temperature
⅓ cup sugar
4 egg yolks
1 teaspoon vanilla
2 cups flour
1 teaspoon baking powder

FILLING
3 tablespoons soft jam
1½ cups chopped nuts — hazelnuts or almonds (or coconut)
1 cup chocolate chips

MERINGUE
4 egg whites
¾ cup sugar

Preparing the dough: In a bowl, mix the margarine and the sugar well. Stir in egg yolks, vanilla, flour, and baking powder. Work into a soft dough.

Lightly flour a 9x11-inch pan. Line it evenly with the dough.

Bake in a preheated oven at 350°F (180°C) for about 15 minutes; the cake will be partially baked.

Preparing the filling: Spread jam over the partially baked dough. In a bowl, stir together the nuts and chocolate. Spread the mixture over the jam layer.

Instead, you can use a mixture of coconut and chocolate.

Preparing the meringue: In a separate bowl, beat the egg whites until peaks are firm, gradually adding the remaining sugar. Gently spread the beaten egg white mixture over the filling. For easier spreading, first place evenly spaced heaping tablespoons of the mixture on the filling. Then spread the mounds into an even, smooth layer with a knife.

Return pan to oven and bake another 30 minutes at 300°F (160°C) until the meringue is lightly browned.

Flaky Almond Slices

Wonderful slices of crispy dough and a sweet layer of almonds or hazelnuts. Adorning this cake is a dusting of powdered sugar. This cake freezes well.

DOUGH

3½ cups flour

2 teaspoons baking powder

1 cup salted margarine, cut into 8 cubes

1 egg

½ cup sugar

1 teaspoon vanilla

scant ¼ cup orange juice or water

FILLING

2 tablespoons soft jam

1 cup ground almonds

½ cup sugar

1 orange — juice and finely grated peel

TOPPING

powdered sugar

Preparing the cake: Sift flour and baking powder into a bowl. Add the margarine, and begin to work into pea-sized pieces of the dough. Add egg, sugar, vanilla, and liquid. Knead dough until it is pliable and easy to roll out. Shape it into a ball.

☕ Lightly flour a 9x11-inch baking pan. Divide the ball of dough into two. Line the baking pan with one portion of the dough, pressing it to form an even layer.

Preparing the filling: Spread jam over the dough. In a bowl, stir together the almonds, sugar, and grated orange peel. Spread this mixture evenly over the jam. Drizzle orange juice over almond layer.

☕ Lightly flour a work surface. Roll the remaining portion of the dough to fit the baking pan. Cover the almond filling with the rolled-out dough. Mark the dough for rectangular slices. Bake the cake in a 375°F (190°C) oven for about 35–40 minutes until nicely browned. Remove the cake from the oven. Sprinkle powdered sugar over the top.

☕ This cake is best when served fresh.

NUT CAKES

Wonderful Nut Cassata

Every bit of a slice of this nut cake brings you a rich, full-bodied taste. Though not high, this attractive cake is of the highest quality. The cake has three layers: a light-colored nut layer, a brown nut layer, and a chocolate frosting. Small squares of this cake served on a white background are especially striking at family celebrations. This cake freezes well.

DOUGH

2 cups flour

2 teaspoons baking powder

½ packet dry yeast

1 cup salted margarine, cut into 8 pieces

1¼ cups sugar

2 cups hazelnuts, ground

2 eggs

rind of one lemon, finely grated

2 tablespoons cocoa powder — for the brown layer

GLAZE

2 tablespoons cocoa powder

1 teaspoon instant coffee

3 tablespoons sugar

about ⅓ cup water

¼ cup unsalted margarine

♔ Dissolve yeast in 2 tablespoons lukewarm water.

♔ Sift flour and baking powder into a large bowl. Add dissolved yeast. Begin to knead the dough while adding the margarine, sugar, nuts, eggs, and lemon rind. Knead well until you have a soft dough — no additional liquid is necessary.

♔ Lightly flour a 9x12-inch ovenproof pan.

♔ Divide the ball of dough into two unequal parts: one-third and two-thirds. Line the baking pan with the larger portion of the dough, pressing evenly.

♔ Place the smaller portion of dough into a bowl; add the cocoa, and mix with the dough until it becomes brown. Divide the brown dough into small portions, and distribute them evenly over the lighter dough.

♔ Bake in a preheated oven at 350°F (180°C) for about 40 minutes. Insert a toothpick to check if done. It is ready when the toothpick comes out clean.

Preparing the frosting: Put cocoa, instant coffee, sugar, and water into a saucepan. Place over medium heat and stir, bringing mixture to a boil. Turn off the flame. Add this syrup to the margarine, and mix thoroughly until smooth.

☞ Pour the frosting over the warm cake. Cool and refrigerate for several hours. Then cut into squares or into narrow wafer-like strips.

NUT CAKES

Elegant Nut Cake, p. 6

Nut and Poppy Seed Kindel

The kindel is a typical pastry from the Hungarian-Jewish kitchen for Purim and Simchas Torah, made from a thinly rolled dough and an outstanding, rich filling of nuts or poppy seed. Kindel can be stored for weeks in the pantry, even without freezing.

DOUGH (FOR 5 ROLLS)

7 cups flour
1 packet yeast
juice and grated rind of one orange
juice and grated rind of one lemon
2 eggs
2 egg yolks
2 cups unsalted margarine
½ cup vegetable oil
5 tablespoons sugar
1 heaping tablespoon honey

NUT FILLING (FOR 1 ROLL)

2 tablespoons honey
¾ cup walnuts, finely chopped
about ½ cup sugar
¼ cup raisins
1 tablespoon grated lemon rind
1 level tablespoon oil

POPPY SEED FILLING (FOR 1 ROLL)

2 tablespoons good-quality jam
1½ cups ground poppy seed
about ½ cup sugar
½ lemon — juice and finely grated rind
¼ cup raisins
1 level tablespoon oil

GLAZE

1 egg, beaten
powdered sugar

Preparing the dough: Sift the flour into a bowl. Dissolve yeast in the juice. Make a well in the flour, and pour the dissolved yeast into it. Add the other ingredients. Knead the dough until elastic and easy to roll out. The amount of liquid you use may change according to the elasticity of the dough. Shape the dough into a ball. Wrap it in waxed paper or a dishtowel, and refrigerate for two hours.

☙ Flour a work surface well. Remove dough from refrigerator and divide it into five balls. Line a 15x10-inch baking pan with baking parchment. Roll out each ball to a thin sheet — one edge should measure 15 inches. The other will take its shape from being rolled out. Kindel is special because when you eat it, you bite into the rich filling and barely feel the dough.

Preparing the nut filling: Spread a thin sheet of dough with honey. In a bowl, mix the nuts, sugar, raisins, and lemon rind. Sprinkle the mixture over the honey. Drizzle oil over the mixture, distributing it evenly. Roll the dough in jelly-roll fashion, and place it in the baking pan. In one large pan, you can bake three nut rolls, keeping them an inch or two apart.

Preparing the poppy seed filling: In a bowl mix the poppy seed, sugar, lemon juice and rind, and raisins. Spread the jam evenly on a thin sheet of dough. Sprinkle the poppy seed mixture over the jam. Drizzle the oil evenly over the mixture. Roll up jelly-roll fashion, and place it in the baking pan. In one large pan you should bake only two poppy seed rolls, since the poppy seed filling seeps out a bit during baking.

☙ Brush beaten egg over the rolls, and make diagonal cuts about ½-inch apart in the top of the dough. Bake the kindel rolls in a preheated 350°F (180°C) oven for 30 minutes or until deep brown.

☙ Just before serving, sprinkle with powdered sugar.

NUT CAKES

Wonderful Nut Cake Layers

A special, beautiful, rich cake. Composed of two layers: a brown base and a speckled layer. A chocolate glaze is the finish for this cake, which fits the bill for a festive occasion when you need a large cake. This cake freezes well.

BASE LAYER

5 eggs, separated

6 tablespoons sugar

1 teaspoon vanilla sugar

½ cup salted margarine, at room temperature

4 ounces bittersweet chocolate, grated fine

1 cup walnuts, ground

3 heaping tablespoons bread crumbs

SPECKLED TORTE

8 eggs, separated

12 tablespoons sugar

2 teaspoons vanilla

1 lemon — juice and grated rind

1½ cups ground hazelnuts

1 tablespoons oil

4 tablespoons self-rising flour

CHOCOLATE GLAZE

2 tablespoons cocoa powder

½ cup sugar

2 tablespoons rum or liqueur

¼ to ⅓ cup water

½ cup unsalted margarine, cubed

Preparing the base: Beat the egg yolks with 2 tablespoons sugar and vanilla. Continue to mix while adding soft margarine, chocolate, and nuts.

In a separate bowl, beat the egg whites while gradually adding the remaining sugar. Fold egg yolk mixture into beaten whites. Gently stir in the bread crumbs.

Line a 9x13-inch baking pan with baking parchment. Pour the brown batter into the pan; smooth the top gently with a spatula.

Preparing the speckled torte: Beat egg yolks in a bowl while adding 4 tablespoons of sugar, lemon (juice and rind), nuts, and oil.

In a separate bowl, beat the egg whites until peaks are firm, while gradually adding the remaining sugar. Gently add the beaten egg whites to the egg yolk mixture. Thoroughly fold the flour into the mixture.

Pour this batter over the base layer.

Bake in a preheated oven at 350°F (180°C) for about 45 minutes. Insert toothpick to test if done. If toothpick comes out clean, cake is ready.

Preparing the glaze: Combine cocoa powder and sugar in a small pan. Add the liquids while stirring. Heat over a low flame, stirring constantly, until all ingredients have melted and a syrup forms. Turn off stove; remove from heat and add the margarine pieces. Stir briskly until you have a smooth, velvety glaze. Pour the glaze over the cake.

Refrigerate cake until served.

NUT CAKES

Linzertorte

Originally stemming from Austria, this cake has a flaky crust-like pastry base, not a light, airy one like sponge cakes. It contains no eggs and is enriched with almonds. A lattice top covers the filling. This cake freezes well.

DOUGH

4 cups flour

3 teaspoons baking powder

1 cup sugar

2 cups salted margarine, cubed

1 tablespoon rum flavoring

1 tablespoon grated lemon rind

1 cup ground almonds or walnuts

about ½ cup juice or water

FILLING

5 heaping tablespoons high-quality jam

½ cup nuts, coarsely chopped

Sift flour and baking powder into a bowl. Add sugar and margarine, and begin to work into a dough. Continue to knead while adding the rum flavor, lemon rind, nuts, and liquid. Knead until you have a uniform, soft dough.

Lightly grease a 9x13-inch pan. Divide dough into two unequal parts, one-third and two-thirds. Put the larger portion into the pan, pressing it evenly to the edges.

Spread the jam evenly over the dough. Sprinkle the coarsely chopped nuts over the jam. Lightly flour a work surface. Roll out the smaller portion of the dough to the size of the baking pan. Cut into strips ½-inch wide. Arrange as a lattice top over the jam layer. Bake in a preheated oven at 350°F (180°C) for about 45 minutes until nicely golden.

Nut Bits

A light, tasty cake with a whipped nut filling. Topping the cake is a layer of crispy, coarsely grated nuts. This cake freezes well.

DOUGH

2 cups salted margarine, at room temperature

1 cup sugar

8 egg yolks

1 teaspoon vanilla

4½ cups of flour

4 teaspoons baking powder

FILLING

4 tablespoons soft jam

8 egg whites

1 cup sugar

1½ cups finely chopped nuts

1 tablespoon cocoa powder

Preparing the dough: In a bowl, mix soft margarine and sugar. Stir in egg yolks and vanilla. Add flour and baking powder. Knead and work into pea-sized pieces of dough. Form into a ball.

Lightly grease a 9x13-inch pan. Divide the dough into two equal parts. Spread one part in the baking pan; use your fingers to stretch the layer evenly. Put the second part of the dough into the freezer for 15 minutes.

Preparing the filling: Spread the jam over the base layer. Beat the egg whites until stiff peaks form, while gradually adding the sugar. By hand, stir into the beaten egg whites the nuts and the cocoa. Spread egg white mixture over the jam. Using a coarse grater, grate the second part of the dough over the jam, arranging the crumbs evenly over the surface.

Bake in a preheated 350°F (180°C) oven for 45 minutes or until lightly browned.

CHEESECAKES are a favorite of many. Indeed, to accommodate all their fans, the possibilities for cheesecakes are plenty. These are light, delicate cakes that can fit any situation; an enriched dairy yeast dough or a flaky-leafed strudel with a cheese filling. There are thin, crispy bases or sponge-cake bases topped with a layer of cheese or a light layer with a creamy mixture. The cheese layer can be hidden in a pastry "sandwich" or decorated with a chocolate glaze, whipped cream frosting, or festive toppings. Cheese fillings can also be used without baking. Combinations of cookies, cheese, and whipped cream match their baked counterparts in taste and quality. *The* holiday for various dairy dishes is Shavuos. However, it is customary to serve dairy dishes on Chanukah as well.

Cheesecakes

Cheese Layer Cake

This cake is a classic. It is possible to bake it using this recipe with two layers of flaky pastry sitting atop a high, whipped cheese layer. For variation one can bake a flaky base with an identical lattice of dough on top or with a topping of baked crumbs. Atop all comes a sprinkle of powdered sugar. This cake freezes well.

DOUGH

3 cups flour

2 teaspoons baking powder

½ ounce dry yeast

½ cup soda water or orange juice

¾ cup salted margarine, cubed

2 egg yolks

2 tablespoons sugar

pinch of salt

FILLING

15 ounces farmer cheese

1 pound cream cheese

5 egg yolks

about 1 cup sugar

2 tablespoons vanilla sugar

1 tablespoon vanilla extract

½ teaspoon cinnamon — optional

2 tablespoons flour

7 egg whites

DECORATION

powdered sugar

Preparing the dough: Sift flour and baking powder into a bowl. Soften the yeast in the liquid, and add to the flour. Add the pieces of margarine, egg yolks, sugar, and salt. Knead and work into a soft, pliable dough that is easy to handle. Wrap the dough, and refrigerate for an hour.

Lightly grease a 9x13-inch pan. Take dough out of refrigerator, and place on a floured work surface; divide into two equal portions. Roll one half to the size of the baking pan. Lift carefully with the rolling pin, and place in the baking pan.

Preheat oven to 350°F (180°C), and bake for about 15 minutes. While dough is baking, prepare the filling.

Preparing the filling: Place the cheeses in a large bowl. Add egg yolks, ½ cup of sugar, vanilla (or cinnamon — as you like), and flour. Stir until thoroughly mixed.

In a separate bowl, beat egg whites with the remaining sugar until stiff peaks form. Fold beaten whites into cheese mixture.

Remove the baking pan from the oven. Pour the whipped cheese mixture over the half-baked dough.

Roll the second part of the dough to a size somewhat larger than the baking pan (it will shrink a bit while baking). Carefully place it over the cheese; prick in several places.

Return the pan to the oven, and bake another 45 minutes. Turn off oven, and let cake remain in it for another 15 minutes. Remove from oven.

Sprinkle powdered sugar over top of cake.

CHEESECAKES

Layered Cheesecake in Puff Pastry

A light, attractive cheesecake. The rich cheese filling is baked between layers of flaky puff pastry. Powdered sugar tops it all. By the way, puff pastry is good for any "sandwich" cake calling for flaky layers. This cake freezes well.

DOUGH I

2 cups flour

2 tablespoons sugar

2 tablespoons vinegar

2 egg yolks

pinch of salt

about ½ cup water

DOUGH II

2 cups flour

1 cup salted margarine, cubed

about ¼ cup water

FILLING

15 oz. farmer cheese

1 pound cream cheese

¾ cup sour cream

1 teaspoon vanilla

1 to 1½ cups sugar (according to taste)

½ lemon — juice and finely grated rind

6 eggs, separated

2 egg whites

3 tablespoons semolina or cornstarch

DECORATION

powdered sugar

Preparing Dough I: Sift flour into a bowl. Add sugar, vinegar, egg yolks, salt, and water. Combine the ingredients into a soft dough, easy to roll out. Adjust the amount of liquid as necessary. On a floured work surface, roll out the dough as thinly as possible.

Preparing Dough II: Sift the flour into a bowl. Cut in the cubed margarine and add the water, working the ingredients together until you have a pliable, uniform dough. Divide the dough into three parts.

☞ Spread one of the parts of Dough II over the rolled out Dough I. Fold opposite edges of the dough towards the middle; the dough will have a long, narrow, rectangular shape. Then fold the long ends of the rectangle toward the middle, one section overlapping the other. Cover the dough with plastic wrap, and refrigerate for 10 minutes.

☞ Remove the dough from the refrigerator, and place on a floured work surface. Roll the dough again to a large sheet. Spread the second portion of Dough II on top of it. Fold as in previous step, and refrigerate for 10 minutes. Repeat the process with the third portion of Dough II. Your puff pastry is now ready.

☞ Divide the puff pastry into two equal parts. Roll out one part to fit a 9x13-inch pan. Lightly grease the pan, and line it with the dough. Prick the dough in several places with a fork to prevent it from puffing up during baking. Bake the dough at 400°F (200°C) for about 15 minutes until lightly browned.

Preparing the filling: Put the cheeses into a bowl. Add the sour cream, vanilla, half the sugar, lemon, and 6 yolks. Stir briskly until thoroughly mixed.

☞ Put egg whites in a mixing bowl. Add the two additional egg whites. Beat whites until stiff, gradually adding the remaining sugar. Fold beaten whites into the cheese mixture.

☞ Gently fold in the semolina or cornstarch. Taste; add additional sugar if necessary. Pour the cheese filling over the baked pastry layer.

☞ Roll out the remaining portion of dough until it is a bit larger than the baking pan. Place this dough over the cheese filling. Prick it in several places with a fork.

☞ Return baking pan to oven, and continue to bake for about 15 minutes at 400°F (200°C). Then lower heat to 350°F (180°C), and bake another 45 minutes.

☞ Before serving, sprinkle powdered sugar over the cake.

Classic Italian Cheesecake

A delightful, rich, beautiful cake. The base of the cake is a thin, flaky pastry; the fruit-filled cheese filling is high, and the top is latticed pastry. Freezes well.

DOUGH

1½ cups flour

½ cup butter or margarine, cubed

4 egg yolks

3 tablespoons dry red wine

3 tablespoons sugar

pinch of salt

1 teaspoon finely grated lemon rind

FILLING

15 oz. farmer cheese

8 ounces cream cheese

¾ cup sour cream OR

　　½ cup sweet cream

1 to 1½ cups sugar

pinch of salt

1 heaping tablespoon flour

1 teaspoon vanilla

rind of one orange, finely grated

4 egg yolks

2 tablespoons raisins

2 tablespoons candied orange peel

8 egg whites

DECORATION

about 20 almonds

1 egg, beaten

Preparing the dough: Sift flour into a bowl. Cut the margarine into the flour, and then add the other ingredients for the dough. Work them together until you have a soft, pliant dough. Shape into a ball, and refrigerate for one hour.

♔ Lightly grease a 10-inch round cake pan. Separate about a quarter of the dough, and set aside for the lattice top. Line the baking pan evenly with the remaining dough.

👨‍🍳 Heat the oven to 350°F, and bake the base layer for about 15 minutes until lightly golden (it will be half-baked).

Preparing the filling: Put the cheeses, cream (sour or sweet), ½ cup sugar, salt, flour, vanilla, orange peel, egg yolks, raisins, and candied peel into a bowl. Stir well until the mixture is uniform.

👨‍🍳 In a separate bowl, beat the egg whites until stiff, gradually adding the remaining sugar. Using broad strokes, fold beaten egg whites into cheese mixture. Pour the light, airy cheese mixture over the half-baked base.

Preparing the lattice top: On a lightly floured surface, roll out the remaining quarter of the dough into a rectangle ¼-inch thick. Cut the dough into narrow strips, ½-inch wide. Place the strips in a latticed pattern over the cheese layer. Put almonds in the spaces between the dough. Spread beaten egg on the latticed dough.

👨‍🍳 Return baking pan to the 350°F (180° C) oven, and bake for an additional 70 minutes. Use a toothpick to check if done. When cake is baked, turn off oven, and leave cake in it for 15 minutes with the oven door open.

👨‍🍳 Refrigerate until served.

Variation: The original Italian recipe does not use egg whites. Increase the amount of farmer cheese to 1½ pounds, and mix all ingredients thoroughly. Whichever variation you use, both cakes are terrific.

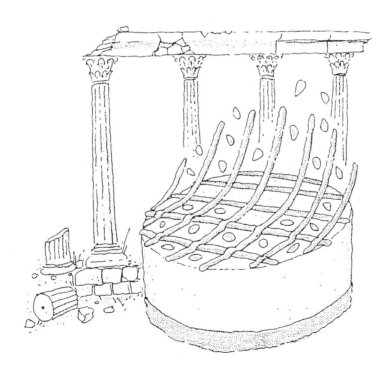

CHEESECAKES

Lattice Cheesecake

A light, rich cheesecake with a flaky base and a lattice top. Powdered sugar gives it that extra touch. This cake freezes well.

DOUGH

3 cups flour

4 teaspoons baking powder

1 cup salted margarine, cubed

¾ cup sour cream

3 tablespoons sugar

finely grated rind of ½ lemon

FILLING

15 oz. farmer cheese

1 pound cream cheese

1½ cups sugar

4 eggs

2 teaspoons vanilla extract

grated rind of 1 lemon

2 tablespoons flour

TOPPING

1 egg yolk

1 tablespoon water

powdered sugar

Preparing the dough: Sift flour and baking powder into a bowl. Add cubed margarine, sour cream, sugar, and lemon rind. Knead into a soft, pliable dough. Refrigerate for 30 minutes. Lightly flour a 9x13-inch baking pan. Set aside a third of the dough for the lattice top. Press remaining dough into pan. Bake in a preheated oven at 350°F (180°C) for about 15 minutes.

Preparing the filling: Put the cheeses into a bowl. Stir in sugar, eggs, vanilla, lemon rind, and flour. Mix until smooth. Remove pan from oven, and pour filling into the partially baked dough.

Preparing the topping: On a floured surface, roll the reserved third of the dough into a rectangle the size of the baking pan. Cut it into ½-inch wide diagonal strips. Lay the strips over the filling in lattice form. In a small bowl, beat the yolk with the water, and brush over the strips.

☕ Return the pan to the oven, and continue to bake for another 45 minutes at 350°F (180°C). Turn off oven. Let baked cake stand in oven for 15 minutes to prevent sinking.

☕ Sprinkle powdered sugar over top.

One-Bowl Cheesecake

A tasty, easy to prepare cheesecake. You just stir all ingredients in a bowl and pour the mixture into a baking pan. This cake can be made richer by adding candied fruits, raisins, or nuts. This cake freezes well.

1 cup margarine or butter, at room temperature
1 cup sugar
1 teaspoon vanilla
8 oz. cream cheese
4 oz. farmer cheese
4 eggs
½ lemon — juice and grated rind
⅓ cup raisins — optional
¼ cup walnuts, broken into pieces — optional
3 cups flour
3 teaspoons baking powder

☕ Place all ingredients in a bowl, and mix into a smooth, soft batter.

☕ Lightly grease two 9x5-inch pans. Pour batter into the two pans. Smooth the top of the batter with a spatula.

☕ Preheat oven to 350°F (180°C), and bake cakes for 50 minutes until lightly browned. Check if cake is done by inserting a toothpick. If it comes out clean, the cake is ready.

Light Airy Cheesecake

A large, rich cake. The thin, flaky base is covered with a rich sour-cream filling containing beaten egg whites. This cake freezes well.

DOUGH

2 cups flour

2 teaspoons baking powder

3 egg yolks

½ cup salted margarine, cubed

⅓ cup sour cream

3 tablespoons sugar

3 to 4 tablespoons orange juice

FILLING

1 pound farmer cheese

1½ pounds cream cheese

1¼ cups sour cream

2 teaspoons vanilla

1½ cups sugar

3 eggs, separated

3 egg whites

3 tablespoons cornstarch

Preparing the dough: Sift flour and baking powder into a bowl. Add egg yolks (use the whites for the filling). Add cubed margarine, sour cream, sugar, and as much juice as necessary. Mix and work into a soft, pliable dough.

☕ Lightly grease a 15x10-inch baking pan. Spread the dough in the pan by hand. Bake at 350°F (180°C) for 15–20 minutes until half baked and lightly browned. (Make the filling while the dough is baking.)

Preparing the filling: Put the cheeses into a bowl. Add sour cream, vanilla, ½ cup sugar, and egg yolks. Mix until all ingredients are combined evenly. Stir in the cornstarch. In a separate bowl, while gradually adding the remaining sugar, beat egg whites until stiff. Gently fold beaten egg whites into cream cheese mixture.

☕ Remove the baking pan from the oven, and pour the filling over the half-baked dough. Return the pan to the oven, and bake at 300°F (160°C) for about 2 hours.

☕ Turn off oven, and let cake stand in the oven, with the door open, for 20 minutes.

Cheese and Crumb Cake

A large, great-tasting cheesecake. The flaky base and whipped filling are topped by a crumb layer. This cake freezes well.

DOUGH

1 cup salted margarine, at room temperature

1 cup sugar

1 teaspoon vanilla

1 egg

4 cups flour

3 teaspoons baking powder

FILLING

15 oz. farmer cheese

1 pound cream cheese

1 package vanilla instant pudding mix

5 eggs, separated

about 1¼ cups sugar

rind of 1 lemon, finely grated

⅓ cup raisins — optional

Preparing the dough: Beat the softened margarine with the sugar. Stir in vanilla, egg, flour, and baking powder. Mix well, and knead into soft dough. Divide dough into two unequal parts, one-third and two-thirds. Put smaller portion in the freezer. Refrigerate larger portion for 30 minutes.

♀ Lightly grease a 15x10-inch baking pan. Spread refrigerated dough evenly in the pan, pressing it until it fills the pan.

♀ Bake in a preheated oven at 350°F (180°C) for 15 minutes until half-baked and golden.

Preparing the filling: Put the cheese into a bowl, stir in the pudding mix, the egg yolks, ½ cup sugar, the lemon rind, and the raisins.

♀ In a separate bowl, beat egg whites with remaining sugar. Gently fold beaten egg whites into the cheese mixture. Pour filling over the layer.

♀ Remove dough from the freezer. Grate the dough into coarse crumbs over the filling. Continue to bake at 350°F (180°C) for an hour until the crumbs are lightly browned. Turn off oven, and let cake stand in it for 20 minutes.

Festive Cheese Pie, p. 48; Cheese Tarts p. 56; Cheese Wraps, p. 58

Excellent Cheesecake

A delightful cake, rich in light cheese, made with a flaky, thin baked base and garnished with a glistening sour cream topping. This cake freezes well.

DOUGH

1 to 1½ cups self-rising flour

½ cup salted margarine

2 eggs

2 tablespoons sugar

FILLING

1 pound cream cheese

15 ounces farmer cheese

1½ to 2 cups sugar

2 teaspoons vanilla extract

8 eggs, separated

½ cup self-rising flour

TOPPING

1½ cups sour cream

2 tablespoons sugar

2 teaspoons vanilla extract OR

    2 tablespoons vanilla sugar

Preparing the dough: Mix all ingredients in a bowl until dough is soft. You can bake this cake in a 9x13-inch baking pan or in a 10-inch round pan. Lightly grease the pan. With floured hands, press the dough into the pan. Bake in a preheated oven at 350°F (180°C) for 10 minutes; the dough will be partially baked.

Preparing the filling: Put the cheeses into a bowl. Stir in 1 cup sugar, vanilla, and egg yolks. In a separate bowl, beat egg whites until firm, while gradually adding the remaining sugar. Gently fold beaten egg whites into the cheese mixture, then fold in flour.

Pour filling over partially baked base layer. Continue to bake at 350°F (180°C) for 1 hour. Remove cake from the oven, and turn off the heat.

Preparing the topping: Put the sour cream into a bowl. Stir in sugar and vanilla. Gently spread topping on the baked filling. Return baking pan to the oven, and let the cake stand in the closed oven for 30 minutes. The sour cream will become a velvety, delicate topping.

Decorated Cheese Torte

An easy-to-make, light-textured cake that is especially tasty. The whipped topping can be decorated with fresh fruits, such as kiwi or strawberries, or with canned fruit. This cake does not freeze well.

TORTE

8 eggs, separated

1¼ cups sugar

1½ cups plain yogurt

15 oz. farmer cheese

1 pound cream cheese

½ package instant vanilla pudding mix

8 tablespoons cornstarch

½ teaspoon baking powder

TOPPING

1 cup whipping cream

2 tablespoons sugar

½ package instant vanilla pudding mix

fresh or canned fruit — optional

Preparing the cake: Beat egg yolks with ¼ cup sugar. Stir in yogurt, cheeses, pudding mix, cornstarch, and baking powder.

In a separate bowl, beat egg whites until stiff, gradually adding the remaining sugar.

Line a 9x11-inch pan with baking parchment. Extend edge of paper beyond rim of pan to help support cake.

Bake at 375°F (190°C) for about 10 minutes. Lower temperature to 350°F (180°C), and bake another 50 minutes, until nicely browned. Turn off oven, and let the cake stand in it with the door open for about another 20 minutes.

Preparing the topping: Pour whipping cream, sugar, and pudding mix into a bowl, and beat with an electric mixer until you have a smooth, delicate whip. Spread it over the cake. Decorate the cake with colorful pieces of fresh or canned fruit, as you choose.

CHEESECAKES

Dairy Crumb Cake

A simple, choice cake, a taste-treat loved by all. The dough is made with cheese, and atop all sits a scrumptious crumb layer. The quantity given here is good for two long, narrow baking forms. For two higher cakes with the same dimensions as these, increase all amounts one and a half times. This cake freezes well.

CAKE

1 cup salted margarine, at room temperature

1 cup sugar

2 teaspoons vanilla extract

8 ounces cream cheese

3 eggs

2 cups flour

2 teaspoons baking powder

CRUMB TOPPING

¼ cup salted margarine

2 tablespoons sugar

½ teaspoon cinnamon

4 heaping tablespoons flour

Preparing the cake: In a bowl, beat softened margarine and sugar. Stir in vanilla sugar, cheese, and eggs, combining well. Fold in flour and baking powder with broad strokes.

Lightly grease two 9x5-inch loaf pans. Pour half the batter into each pan. Smooth top with spatula.

Preparing the crumbs: Mix margarine, sugar, cinnamon, and flour. Work with fingers into crumb-size pieces. Sprinkle evenly over the cake.

Bake in a preheated oven at 350°F (180°C) for one hour until lightly browned.

Cheese Pie

The base is a thin piecrust. The tasty filling consists of cheese and a sour cream layer. This pie freezes well.

DOUGH (FOR 2 CRUSTS)
2 cups flour
1 cup salted margarine, cubed
½ cup powdered sugar
½ teaspoon vanilla extract
1 teaspoon grated lemon rind
3 tablespoons water

FILLING
15 ounces farmer cheese
8 ounces cream cheese
¼ cup salted margarine, at room temperature
1¼ cups sugar
3 eggs
1 teaspoon vanilla
2 tablespoons cornstarch
½ lemon — juice and grated rind

TOPPING
1½ cups sour cream
2 teaspoons vanilla extract
2 tablespoons sugar

Preparing piecrust: Sift flour into a bowl. Add margarine. Work into a stiff dough while adding the other ingredients.

♟ Lightly grease a 10-inch round pan. Line it evenly with half the dough. Bake at 350°F (180°C) for about 15 minutes until lightly browned. It will be partially baked.

Preparing the filling: Put the cheeses in a bowl. Mix in the margarine, sugar, eggs, vanilla, cornstarch, and lemon juice and rind. Pour the mixture over the crust. Continue to bake at 350°F (180°C) for about 1 hour more.

Preparing the topping: In a bowl, mix the sour cream, vanilla, and sugar. Pour over the cheese layer, and bake for 10 minutes more. Turn off oven. Cool cake in the partialy-opened oven for 20 minutes. Refrigerate until served.

CHEESECAKES

Festive Cheese Pie [picture on page 42]

The only word for this pie is marvelous! The base is made from finely ground cookie crumbs. You bite into a high cheese layer made richer with sour cream, beaten egg whites, and pudding — and in addition to a tasty whipped cream top. Wonderful to serve on Shavuos. This pie freezes well.

CRUST

2 cups cookie crumbs, finely ground

½ cup softened butter or margarine

½ teaspoon grated lemon rind — optional

FILLING

15 ounces farmer cheese

8 ounces cream cheese

¾ cup sour cream

¾ cup plain yogurt

1 tablespoon vanilla

6 heaping tablespoons flour

6 eggs, separated

1½ cups sugar

½ package instant vanilla pudding mix

TOPPING

1 cup whipping cream

1 cup milk

½ package instant vanilla pudding mix

Preparing the crust: Combine cookie crumbs with margarine and lemon rind. Lightly grease an 11-inch round pan or a 9x13-inch baking pan. Press the crumbs into the pan evenly.

Preparing the filling: Put the cheeses into a bowl. Add sour cream, yogurt, and vanilla. Stir in flour and egg yolks.

In a separate bowl, beat egg whites until stiff, gradually adding remaining sugar. Continue to beat; add pudding mix. Fold beaten egg whites into cheese mixture. Pour over the crust. Bake at 350°F (180°C) for about 60 minutes. Turn off oven; let cake stand in it to cool for 20 minutes.

Preparing the topping: Put the whipping cream, milk, and pudding mix into a bowl. Beat into a firm, but not stiff, topping. Spread over the cooled cheese pie. Refrigerate for several hours. The frosting becomes stiff enough to slice.

No-Bake Cheesecake

A light, impressive, no-fuss cake. This cake consists of three layers of cookies separated by a chocolate cheese filling. A chocolate glaze tops it all. Freezes well.

About 105 plain cookies or cookies for ice-cream sandwiches.
About ½ cup sweet wine

FILLING

15 ounces farmer cheese
1 pound cream cheese
1½ cups sour cream
1 cup whipping cream
1 cup milk
1 package instant chocolate pudding mix
1 cup sugar

GLAZE

2 tablespoons cocoa
½ cup sugar
⅓ cup water
1 tablespoon rum flavoring or wine
½ cup unsalted margarine, cubed

♕ Line a 15x10-inch pan with baking parchment that extends beyond rim of pan. Dip 35 cookies in wine, and arrange them in the baking pan as the bottom layer of the cake.

Preparing the filling: Put cheeses and sour cream into a bowl; mix well. Put whipping cream, milk, and chocolate pudding mix into bowl of mixer. Beat pudding until smooth. Gently add to cheese. Add sugar, and beat until well mixed and smooth.

♕ Cover the cookie base with half the filling. Arrange a second layer of cookies over the filling. Spread the remaining filling over the cookies, and top with remaining cookies.

Preparing the glaze: Put cocoa and sugar into a sauce pan. Stir in liquids. Melt over medium heat, stirring constantly with a wooden spoon. Remove from heat, and add margarine. Stir until a chocolate syrup forms. Pour the syrup over the top layer of cookies; spread it evenly with a spatula.

♕ Refrigerate until served.

Layered Cheese Festival

The classic cheesecake needs no public relations. This time it comes in impressive, festive garb that makes it better then ever. This cake has a number of layers: a thin, flaky pastry base; a layer of tart, soft apples; a high cheese filling; a top layer rich in whipped cream and pudding; and a chocolate glaze. You can even add chopped nuts or candied cherries. The large, high cake is perfect for serving guests. You can make a smaller version of this cake by decreasing all ingredients by one-third. Use a 10-inch springform pan. This cake freezes well.

DOUGH

2 cups all-purpose flour

2 egg yolks

1 cup margarine

¼ cup sugar

CHEESE FILLING

15 ounces farmer cheese

1½ pounds cream cheese

1½ cups sour cream

5 heaping tablespoons self-rising flour

11 egg yolks

4 teaspoons vanilla extract

2 cups sugar

finely grated rind of 1 lemon

13 egg whites

APPLE LAYER

4 large baking apples

¼ cup sugar

½ lemon — juice and finely grated rind

½ teaspoon vanilla extract

WHIPPED CREAM LAYER

1 cup whipping cream

2 cups milk

2 packages instant vanilla pudding mix

CHOCOLATE GLAZE

6 tablespoons sugar

2 tablespoons cocoa powder

3 tablespoons water

¼ cup margarine

2 ounces bittersweet chocolate

1 tablespoon vanilla extract

TOPPING

½ cup chopped walnuts, OR candied cherries

Preparing the dough: Put all ingredients into a bowl. Knead well by hand or with an electric beater into a soft dough. Lightly grease a 15x10x2-inch baking pan. Line pan with dough. Bake for 10 minutes in a preheated oven at 350°F (180°C), until golden and partially baked.

♟ Remove pan from oven. When cooled, use baking parchment to make a border around the baking pan 2½ to 3 inches high to support the filling.

Preparing the cheese filling: Except for egg whites and ½ cup of the sugar, put all ingredients into a large bowl. Mix well until thoroughly blended.

♟ In a separate bowl, beat egg whites until stiff, gradually adding the ½ cup sugar. Gently fold beaten whites into the cheese mixture. Spread over the partially baked dough.

♟ In this next stage, the cake is baked at two different temperatures. First, preheat oven to 450°F (220°C), and bake for 15 minutes. (Baking for a short time at high temperature helps make the cheese filling stable.) Lower oven to 325°F (170°C) and bake for another 75 minutes. Turn off oven. Let cake stand in it for about 30 minutes to cool and prevent cake from sinking.

Preparing the apple layer: Peel and core apples. Cut into thin slices and put into saucepan. Add sugar, lemon, and vanilla. Cook the apples uncovered over low heat, about 15–20 minutes. The liquids released during cooking will evaporate. Spoon cooked apples over the cake.

Preparing the whipped cream layer: Put whipping cream, milk, and pudding into mixing bowl. Beat until smooth and well blended. Spread over apples.

Preparing the chocolate glaze: In a saucepan, mix sugar, cocoa, and water. While stirring, cook over medium heat until the sugar dissolves and a smooth syrup forms. Remove from heat, and add the margarine and chocolate cut into small pieces. Add vanilla. Pour the glaze and cover the top or drizzle it at random.

♟ At this stage the cake is elegant, impressive, and very tasty. You can add an extra touch by sprinkling broken nuts, candied cherries, and so on over all.

♟ Refrigerate the cake.

Layered Cheese Torte

A light, delectable torte on a flaky base. The quantities listed are for a medium-sized baking pan. If you prefer to use a small round pan, use half the amount of dough for the base and only about one pound of cream cheese. Freezes well.

DOUGH

1 cup salted margarine

2 egg yolks

2 tablespoons sugar

1 tablespoon finely grated lemon rind

1 teaspoon vanilla

2½ cups flour

about 2 tablespoons water

TORTE

¼ cup ground walnuts

6 eggs, separated

2 egg whites

1½ cups sugar

¾ cup sour cream

½ lemon — juice and rind

15 ounces farmer cheese

8 ounces cream cheese

¼ cup raisins

2 tablespoons self-raising flour

Preparing the dough: Cube the margarine and beat until light with egg yolks and sugar. Stir in lemon rind and vanilla. Add flour and water; knead into a soft, pliable dough. The amount of water may change as you work with the dough.

♟ Separate a third of the dough, shape into a ball, and freeze for 15 minutes. Lightly flour a 9x13-inch pan. Line with the remaining dough, pressing it in evenly. Bake at 350°F (180°C) for 15 minutes until partially baked.

Preparing the cake: Sprinkle the nuts over the half-baked base. Put yolks in a bowl. Stir in ¼ cup sugar, sour cream, lemon juice and rind, farmer cheese, cream cheese, raisins, and flour. Mix until well combined.

♟ In a separate bowl, beat egg whites until stiff, gradually adding the remaining sugar. Fold whites into the cheese mixture. Pour the batter over the base. Remove dough from freezer, and grate it over the torte into coarse crumbs. Bake at 350°F (180°C) for 60 minutes. Turn off the oven. Cool cake in the oven for 20 minutes.

Light Cheesecake

A wonderful cheesecake with a light filling. You can bake it in a round pan and cut it into large wedges or use a rectangular pan and serve small squares. This cake freezes well.

CAKE

6 eggs, separated
½ cup sugar
3 tablespoons oil
2 tablespoons cognac
½ lemon — juice and finely grated rind
1½ cups self-rising flour

FILLING

15 ounces farmer cheese
1 pound cream cheese
1 cup sugar
3 teaspoons vanilla

Preparing the cake: Beat well the egg yolks, ¼ cup sugar, oil, cognac, and lemon.

In a separate bowl, beat egg whites until stiff, gradually adding remaining sugar. Gently fold beaten egg whites into yolk mixture. Using broad strokes, fold in flour.

Line a round 11-inch baking pan or a rectangular 9x13-inch pan with baking parchment. Pour a third of the torte batter into the pan. Use a spatula to smooth it evenly.

Bake this base layer about 10 minutes at 350°F (180°C) until lightly browned; it will be partially baked.

Preparing the filling: Put the cheese in a bowl. Add sugar and vanilla. Gently stir in a third of the cake batter (half the remaining amount). Pour this mixture over the base. Carefully spread the remaining cake batter uniformly over the cheese layer.

Return pan to oven, and continue to bake at 350°F (180°C) for 50 minutes. Insert a toothpick to check if done. It is ready when the toothpick comes out clean. Turn off the oven. Let the torte stand in the oven, with its door open, for another 20 minutes to cool.

Sicilian Cheese Cassata

An excellent Italian cake. You can make this using a baked torte or English cake. For an easy variation, use plain cookies. The cassata consists of a number of cake layers with a delicate cheese filling between them, all topped by a luscious frosting. This cake freezes well.

CAKE

Basic Sponge Cake (page 80) OR
    20 thin ice-cream sandwich cookies

FILLING

8 ounces cream cheese

7½ ounces farmer cheese

½ cup sugar

3 tablespoons candied fruits or raisins

3 ounces grated chocolate — optional

1 teaspoon vanilla extract

2 tablespoons orange liqueur

1 cup whipping cream — optional

FROSTING

6 ounces bittersweet chocolate, broken into pieces

½ cup water + 1 teaspoon instant coffee granules

4 tablespoons sugar

¾ cup unsalted margarine, cubed

2 egg yolks

Preparing the cake: Prepare the batter according to recipe instructions for a white, flecked, or dark sponge cake. Divide the batter into two parts, and bake in two long, narrow, baking-parchment lined 5x9-inch pans. Bake for 40 minutes at 350°F (180°C). Cool the cakes, then remove from pans. Using a long, serrated knife, cut each cake widthwise into three or four layers.

If you are using cookies: cover a serving tray with baking parchment. For the cassata base, use five cookies in a row. You may dip them first in milk. The finished cassata will have four layers of cookies with the filling between them.

Preparing the filling (enough for the two loaf cakes): In a bowl, mix the cheese, sugar, fruits, chocolate, vanilla, and liqueur. (If using whipping cream, beat it until firm, adding 1 teaspoon powdered sugar.) Divide the cheese mixture into two bowls.

Assembling each cassata loaf: Spread one third of the cheese mixture on the first sliced layer of cake. Place the second slice of cake over the cheese layer. Spread another third of the cheese mixture over it. Continue with remaining cake and cheese, ending with a cake layer, gently pressing it onto the cream mixture.

☞ If using cookies, assemble the cassata in the same way.

☞ For best results, refrigerate for two hours.

Preparing the frosting: Place the chocolate pieces into a saucepan, and melt over boiling water. Pour the melted chocolate into a blender or processor bowl. Add coffee, water, sugar, margarine, and egg yolks. Blend until you have a smooth, velvety frosting.

☞ Frost top and sides of each cake. You can use chocolate sprinkles, cherries, and so on to decorate the cake.

☞ Refrigerate the cake until served.

Cheese Tarts [picture on page 42]

Cheese cookies are among the best of Hungarian baked goods. The dough is mixed thoroughly and has a flaky texture. The filling is rich in cheese and pudding. The dough squares can be folded over twice and shaped like tarts, or all four edges can be folded over making enveloped cookies, delkelach. Powdered sugar covers the tops. These tarts freeze well.

DOUGH

4 cups flour
1 package dry yeast
about ½ to ¾ cup lukewarm water or milk
1 egg
1 cup margarine or butter
2 tablespoons sugar

FILLING

22½ ounces farmer cheese (3 packages of 7.5 ounces)
2 eggs
1½ cups sugar
1 heaping tablespoon grated lemon rind
1 tablespoon vanilla
½ package instant vanilla pudding mix

TOPPING

1 egg, beaten
powdered sugar

Preparing the dough: Sift flour into a bowl. Dissolve yeast in ½ cup lukewarm water and pour into a well in the flour. Add egg, ½ cup margarine, and sugar. Knead into a pliable dough. The amount of water will have to be adjusted as you work. Shape dough into a ball, and flour it lightly.

♙ Cover with a dishtowel, and let rise 30 minutes.

♙ Liberally flour a work surface. Roll dough into a square, and spread ¼ cup softened margarine on it. Fold in two sides towards the middle, like a book. Fold the right third over the middle, and cover it with the left third. Lightly flour it, and let it stand for another 20 minutes. Roll the dough again, and spread it with the remaining margarine. Repeat the folding as described.

♙ Either allow the dough to stand for another 20 minutes or wrap and refrigerate it until needed.

Preparing the filling: Put the cheese into a bowl. Add eggs, sugar, lemon rind, vanilla, and pudding mix. Stir until smooth. Taste and adjust the flavor, as necessary.

Making the cookies: Divide dough into two. Roll each part into a square about 14 inches by 14 inches, and divide each sheet of dough into 25 squares. Put one heaping teaspoon of filling on each square. Pinch together two opposite corners of each square, and hold together with a toothpick. The other two corners remain open.

Line two cookie sheets with baking parchment. Place the cookies on the tray. Brush them with beaten egg.

Bake each tray at 375°F (190°C) for about 25 minutes until nicely browned.

Before serving, sprinkle with powdered sugar.

Variation: To make "envelopes" — *delkelach*: Divide the dough into 16 squares. Put one heaping teaspoon of filling in the middle of each. Overlap two facing edges of a square. Place a third edge over them, and then cover with the fourth, making an envelope. Pinch the center to firmly close all. Use a toothpick to hold edges closed. Put the *delkelach* on cookie trays.

Brush with beaten egg, and bake at 375°F (190°C) for about 25 minutes.

CHEESECAKES

Cold Yeast Dough Cheese Wraps

[picture on page 42]

Use cold yeast dough also for delkelach. It's best to use firm cheese that won't seep out of the dough cover. These Cheese Wraps freeze well.

DOUGH

Cold Yeast Dough, page 222

FILLING (ENOUGH FOR TWO BALLS OF DOUGH — 18 WRAPS)

15 ounces farmer cheese

1½ cups sugar

1 tablespoon cinnamon

1 egg yolk

⅓ cup raisins — optional

TOPPING

egg white

powdered sugar

Preparing the dough: Prepare one recipe of dough according to the instructions. Separate the dough into six balls. The amount of cheese listed is enough for two balls of dough. If you want to use all the dough for Cheese Wraps, triple the filling accordingly.

♔ Preparing the wraps: Line a cookie tray with baking parchment. Lightly flour a work surface. From each portion of dough, roll a square 12x12 inches. Divide into nine squares each measuring 4 x 4 inches.

♔ Put cream cheese into a bowl. Add sugar (to taste), cinnamon, and egg yolk. Mix until thoroughly blended. Put a heaping tablespoon of filling on each square. Close edges over filling by folding over opposite corners — until filling is wrapped. Pinch all corners together to close well. To prevent opening during baking, insert a toothpick through the corners brought to the center.

♔ Put the wraps on cookie trays, leaving an inch between them. Brush egg white over tops.

♔ Bake for 30 minutes in a preheated oven at 375°F (190°C) until nicely browned.

♔ Before serving, sprinkle with powdered sugar.

AMONG THE LIGHT, delicate cakes, honey cake takes a place of pride. The honey graces the cakes with a light brown tone, adding a special texture loved by all. You can stir candied orange peel or pieces of nuts into the batter to make the cake even richer. Honey cakes are also among the best of creamy tortes. Because of their symbolic sweetness and the biblical phrase "honey and milk under your tongue," referring to Torah learning, honey cakes are an integral part of Rosh Hashanah, Purim, and Shavuos foods.

Honey Cakes

Wonderful Honey Sponge Cake

A large, light, delicious honey sponge cake. If the cake is larger than you need for now, you can freeze part of it to use later. Instead of baking it in one large baking pan, you can use three or four loaf pans. It's great as part of mishlo'ach manos or on any festive occasion. This cake freezes well.

12 eggs, separated
1¼ cups sugar
1¼ cups honey
¾ cups oil
1 tablespoon of instant coffee dissolved in ½ cup hot water
1½ level teaspoons baking soda
1½ teaspoons cinnamon
1½ teaspoons ground cloves
1 teaspoon grated lemon rind
3 cups flour

♗ Put egg yolks into a bowl. Add half the sugar, the honey, oil, coffee, baking soda, cinnamon, cloves, and lemon. Mix until thoroughly combined.

♗ In a different bowl, beat egg whites until firm, gradually adding the other half of the sugar.

♗ Gently combine beaten egg whites with the yolk mixture. Fold in the flour. Line a 9x13-inch baking pan with baking parchment, with the paper extending beyond the rim of the pan.

♗ Bake in a preheated oven at 350°F (180°C) for about 45 minutes. Insert a toothpick to check if ready; if it comes out dry, cake is done.

Festive Honey Cake

An attractive, especially light, delectable honey cake. This recipe gives you a large, elegant cake. Just right for holidays and simchas, it can be baked in advance and frozen or sliced fresh into luscious high, thin servings. This cake freezes well.

6 eggs, separated
3 cups sugar
¾ cup oil
1 teaspoon baking soda
1 level teaspoon ground cloves
1 level teaspoon cinnamon
1 tablespoon cognac
1 tablespoon instant coffee granules
1 cup honey
2¼ cups water
4½ to 5 cups flour
6 teaspoons baking powder

♔ Use a 15x10-inch baking pan or two long, narrow pans.

♔ Put egg yolks into a large bowl. Stir in 2 cups sugar, oil, baking soda, cloves, cinnamon, cognac, instant coffee, honey, and water. Beat well until all ingredients are well blended. In a separate bowl, beat egg whites until stiff, gradually adding 1 cup sugar. Fold beaten egg whites into the batter. With broad strokes, fold in flour and baking powder. Make sure no lumps of flour are in the batter.

♔ Line the baking pan with baking parchment; pour the batter into the pan.

♔ Bake in a preheated oven at 350°F (180°C) for about 70 minutes. Insert a toothpick to check if done. It is ready when the toothpick comes out clean.

Serving tip: Cut the cake into four long strips; slice into narrow, high pieces, each one a delight to serve.

Mixer Honey Cake

A delightful honey cake full of raisins and nuts. Even though this cake is prepared in stages, it is easy to make. When making it for Rosh Hashanah, omit the nuts. This cake freezes well.

½ cup sugar
1 scant tablespoon baking soda
4 tablespoons oil
1 egg
1 cup water
½ cup honey
2 heaping cups flour
⅓ cup raisins, briefly soaked in water
½ cup walnuts, coarsely chopped

☙ Put sugar into a mixer bowl. Add baking soda, oil, and egg, and mix well at medium speed. Pour in ½ cup water and the honey; mix until uniformly blended. Add the flour.

☙ Cover the bowl with a kitchen towel, and let the mixture stand for about 8 hours at room temperature.

☙ Pour in an additional ½ cup of water, and stir in the drained raisins and the nuts.

☙ Lightly grease a 9x5-inch loaf pan. Bake in a preheated oven at 350°F (180°C) for about 40 minutes until nicely browned.

Rich Honey Cake

A delicious honey cake with full-bodied texture. The cake is especially rich with grated apple or bits of nuts (omitted for Rosh Hashanah). This cake freezes well.

4 eggs, separated
¾ cup sugar
¾ cup honey
1 cup oil
1 tablespoon instant coffee dissolved in
1 cup hot water
½ lemon — juice and finely grated rind
½ teaspoon cinnamon
½ teaspoon ground cloves
½ teaspoon baking soda
1 cup apple, coarsely grated, OR
   ½ cup walnuts, finely chopped
3 cups flour

In a bowl, beat egg yolks with ¼ cup sugar. Add and mix well honey, oil, coffee, lemon juice and rind, cinnamon, cloves, and baking soda. Add the apple or nuts.

In a separate bowl, beat egg whites until stiff, gradually adding remaining sugar.

Gently fold beaten egg whites into honey mixture. Using broad strokes, fold in flour.

Lightly grease, or line with baking parchment, a 10-inch round pan. Pour the batter into the pan.

Bake in a preheated oven at 350°F (180°C) for about 1 hour until nicely browned. Insert a toothpick to check if ready; if it comes out dry, cake is done.

Mock Honey Cake

Honey cakes are considered most delicate and delicious. When you do not have natural honey on hand, you can bake a mock honey cake, quite close to the real thing in taste and color. This cake freezes well.

SUGAR SYRUP (CARAMEL)

½ cup sugar

1 tea bag

1 cup boiling water

2 tablespoons jam

CAKE

¼ cup salted margarine, at room temperature

1 cup sugar

3 eggs

2 tablespoons oil

⅓ cup raisins — optional

1 teaspoon baking soda

1 teaspoon ground cloves

1 teaspoon cinnamon

1 teaspoon instant coffee powder

½ lemon — juice and finely grated rind

3 cups flour

Preparing the sugar syrup (caramel): Put the sugar into a flat pan. Soak the tea bag in the boiling water. Melt the sugar over medium heat, until lightly brown. Carefully pour the water over the melted sugar, and turn off the heat. Add the jam while stirring.

Preparing the cake: In a bowl, beat the margarine and sugar. Add eggs, oil, raisins, baking soda, and spices. Combine thoroughly. Beat in the sugar syrup. Using broad strokes, fold in the flour.

♔ Grease, or line with baking parchment, a round 10-inch baking pan. Pour in the batter, and smooth the top with a spatula.

♔ Bake for 45 minutes in a preheated oven at 350°F (180°C) until nicely browned. Insert a toothpick to check if ready; if it comes out dry, cake is done.

HONEY CAKES

DOBOS CAKES are prestigious among Hungarian baked goods. This category includes excellent, beautiful, delicious cakes consisting of a number of layers with fillings between them. The layers can be made from flaky pastry or sponge-cake type tortes. The fillings can be light colored and vanilla flavored, or mocha or chocolate in tone and taste, and so on. Most commonly, chocolate frosting tops these cakes. You can bake Dobos cakes in rectangular pans and serve small square slices or bake them in round pans and cut high, triangular slices. To make things easier, you can buy pre-baked torte layers. Then all you have to do is to make the filling and assemble the cake.

Dobos Cakes

Dairy Caramel Dobos

The Dobos cake is special owing to its tiered structure. It has three layers of flaky pastry separated by two layers of dairy caramel pudding. Chocolate glaze covers the top. You can also use a chocolate frosting (see Index) between the layers. This cake freezes well.

DOUGH

2½ cups flour

1 teaspoon baking powder

1 egg

3 tablespoons sugar

½ cup salted margarine, cubed

about ½ cup juice or water

CARAMEL PUDDING

7 tablespoons sugar

2½ cups milk

3 heaping tablespoons cornstarch

1 tablespoon instant coffee powder

1 tablespoon vanilla extract

½ cup butter or margarine

CHOCOLATE GLAZE

2 tablespoons cocoa

4 tablespoons sugar

4 tablespoons water

1 tablespoon vanilla extract

1 tablespoon unsalted margarine, at room temperature

Preparing the cake layers: Sift flour and baking powder into a bowl. Add egg, sugar, and margarine. Begin to work and knead into a dough, gradually adding the liquid. Continue kneading until the dough is pliable and easy to roll. Divide into three. Lightly flour a work surface. Roll each part of the dough into a 9x13-inch rectangle.

♙ Lightly grease the outside of a 9x13-inch pan. (Bake the layers on the outside of the pan, so it will be easier for you to slide them onto a tray after baking.)

♙ Put a sheet of dough on the greased pan. (Drape dough over rolling pin when moving it.) Bake for about 12 minutes in a preheated 350°F (180°C) oven.

⌇ Carefully transfer the baked dough to a flat tray to prevent breaking.

Preparing the filling: Put 4 tablespoons sugar into a small sauce pan. Melt it over medium heat until you have a golden syrup. Remove pan from heat. While stirring, pour in 2 cups milk, and return pan to stove. Bring to boil. In the meantime, dissolve cornstarch in remaining ½ cup milk; add instant coffee powder. When milk in the pan is boiling, stir in dissolved cornstarch, and continue cooking and stirring until the mixture thickens into a pudding. Turn off stove, and remove pan from heat. Add vanilla, and stir in butter. Stir until pudding is smooth. Let cool a bit.

⌇ Put the first baked layer onto a nice serving tray. Spread half of the pudding over it. Place second baked layer over it, and spread remaining pudding on it. Place third baked layer over pudding.

Preparing the frosting: Put the cocoa, sugar, and water into a saucepan; stir together well. Place over medium heat, and cook until a chocolate syrup forms. Turn off the heat, and add vanilla and margarine. Stir until frosting is smooth. Pour the glaze over the top baked layer.

⌇ Refrigerate until served.

Chocolate Dobos

A classic Dobos composed of torte layers between a chocolate frosting. You can use any flavor frosting you wish. The torte layers can be round or square. This very pretty festive cake is served in small portions. Decorate as you wish. This cake freezes well.

TORTE LAYERS

8 eggs, separated

8 tablespoons sugar

⅓ cup oil

½ lemon — juice and finely grated rind

1 teaspoon vanilla

8 tablespoons self-rising flour

FROSTING

1 tablespoon cocoa

1 teaspoon instant coffee powder

½ cup sugar

¼ cup water

7 ounces chocolate

1 cup unsalted margarine, cubed

2 eggs

3 tablespoons brandy or chocolate liqueur

Preparing torte layers: You can bake them round and cut wedges; or, bake them as squares and cut lovely square pieces, easier to serve at *simchas*. You can also decide on the number of layers. You can bake very thin layers and assemble a cake from six or seven layers. Alternately, you can bake four thicker layers and spread frosting between them.

♧ Beat egg whites with 2 tablespoons sugar. Mix in oil, lemon juice and rind, and vanilla. In a separate bowl, beat the egg whites until stiff, gradually adding the remaining sugar. Gently combine the beaten egg whites with the yolk mixture. Using broad strokes, fold in flour.

♧ ROUND LAYERS: Line an 8-inch round baking pan with baking parchment. Divide the batter according to the number of layers you want to bake. Pour into the pan batter for one layer. Bake for 10 minutes in a preheated 350°F (180°C) oven until nicely golden.

☕ SQUARE LAYERS: Line an 8-inch square pan with baking parchment. Divide the batter according to the number of layers you want to bake. Pour into the pan batter for one layer. Bake for 10 minutes in a preheated 350°F (180°C) oven until nicely golden.

☕ FOR ALL LAYERS: Lightly flour a work surface. Turn the baked layer out onto the floured surface, and peel off the baking parchment. You can bake all layers in the same pan, one after the other.

Preparing the frosting: In a small saucepan mix cocoa, instant coffee powder, and sugar. Mix in ¼ cup water, and bring to boil over medium heat. Break chocolate into pieces, and add to hot syrup. Continue to stir until chocolate melts. Pour syrup into a food processor or blender. Turn on the machine, and add the margarine, eggs, and brandy. Mix well. Refrigerate for an hour.

Assembling the cake: Line a serving tray with a paper doily. Put the first baked layer on the doily. Spread with a thin layer of frosting. Cover it with the second baked layer. Frost the second layer. Continue with remaining layers. Spread frosting on top. Decorate, if you wish. with a candied cherry or half a walnut on each slice.

DOBOS CAKES

Vanilla Dobos

Vanilla Dobos is composed of four flaky pastry layers and vanilla filling. Adding honey to the pastry gives it a richer taste and makes for an interesting variation. Chocolate frosting covers all. This cake freezes well.

DOUGH

4 cups flour
½ teaspoon baking soda
5 tablespoons sugar
3 tablespoons honey
about ½ cup water
¼ cups salted margarine
1 egg

VANILLA PUDDING

1 cup sugar
4 heaping tablespoons flour
2 eggs
2½ cups water
4 teaspoons vanilla extract
1 cup salted margarine, cubed
juice of ½ lemon

CHOCOLATE FROSTING

1 cup sugar
3 heaping tablespoons cocoa
about ⅓ cup water
½ cup unsalted margarine, cubed

Preparing the dough: Sift flour and baking soda into a bowl. Add the remaining ingredients, and knead into a pliable dough, easy to roll out.

♟ Divide the dough into four parts. Lightly grease the outside of a 9x13-inch baking pan. Lightly flour a work surface. Roll out the first portion of dough to the size of the baking pan. Using the rolling pan, place the dough on the outside of the baking pan.

♟ Preheat the oven to 350°F (180°C). Bake the dough for 10 minutes until lightly brown. Carefully move the baked sheet of dough to a tray without edges. Bake the other three portions of dough the same way.

Preparing the vanilla filling: Put sugar, flour, eggs, water, and vanilla into a blender or food processor. Combine evenly. Pour the mixture into a saucepan. Bring to boil over medium heat, stirring constantly with a wooden spoon. When the heated mixture thickens like a pudding, turn off the heat. Add the margarine and the juice. Stir until the pudding is smooth and velvety. Place it in the freezer for 10–15 minutes.

Preparing the chocolate frosting: Put sugar, cocoa, and water into a saucepan. Stirring constantly with a wooden spoon, bring to a boil over medium heat. Turn off heat, and add margarine. Stir until frosting is smooth.

Assembling the cake: Line a pan — the same size as the baked sheets of dough — with baking parchment. Put in the first baked layer and spread a third of the vanilla filling over it. Put the second layer on top of it. Spread another third of filling over it. Cover with the third layer; spread the remaining filling over it. Cover with the fourth layer. Pour chocolate frosting over the fourth layer. Spread it evenly with a spatula.

Refrigerate the cake until serving. We recommend cutting the cake into small squares with a serrated knife.

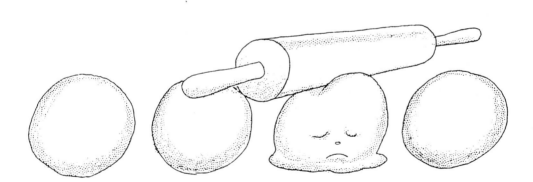

Sour Cream Nut Dobos

A special, light cake. This Dobos has three layers, separately baked, enriched with ground nuts. The filling contains nuts and sour cream. For this recipe use the firmest sour cream (the higher the fat content, the firmer the sour cream). This cake does not freeze well.

DOUGH

1¼ cups margarine or butter
½ cup sugar
2 cups flour
½ cup ground walnuts
1 egg — optional

FILLING

2¼ cups sour cream
2 teaspoons vanilla
½ cup sugar
1½ cups ground walnuts
1 tablespoon cocoa — optional

Preparing the baked layers: In a bowl, beat the margarine and sugar well. Beat in the flour and nuts (and egg). Knead into a uniform dough.

♟ Divide the dough into three parts. You can bake round layers using a 9-inch round pan or rectangular layers using an 8x11-inch pan. Grease the outside of the pan you are using. On a floured surface, roll each portion to a sheet the size of the pan. Put the dough on the greased pan.

♟ Bake each sheet in a preheated 350°F (180°C) oven for 12–15 minutes until lightly golden. Cool and place on a tray. Bake the other two layers the same way.

Preparing the filling: Pour the sour cream into a bowl. Add vanilla, sugar, ground nuts, and cocoa (if you want a dark filling). Mix thoroughly and combine well.

♟ Place a baked layer on a tray. Spread half the filling over it. Cover the filling with the next baked layer. Spread the remaining filling over it. Place the third layer over the filling.

♟ It is also possible to divide the filling into three portions and spread some over the third layer. Sprinkle ground nuts on top.

Nougat Dobos

A lovely, delicious cake that is easily assembled. You buy the wafers ready-made and spread a special chocolate filling on them. The wafer may be round or square. This cake freezes well.

5 or 6 wafer leaves

FILLING

½ cup cocoa powder

1 cup sugar

about ½ cup water

4 ounces halvah

1 tablespoon honey

2 ounces cooking chocolate

½ cup unsalted margarine

½ teaspoon vanilla or rum or liqueur

♙ Put all ingredients for the filling into a sauce pan in the order listed. Mix together. Cook over a medium flame, stirring constantly, until the mixture is smooth.

♙ Put a paper doily on a serving tray. Set a wafer leaf on the doily. Spread part of the frosting on the wafer. Repeat with layer of wafers alternating with filling, ending with a filling layer frosting the top wafer.

♙ Refrigerate until served.

DOBOS CAKES

THESE ARE light cakes that can be decorated to fit any occasion. Their "melt-in-the-mouth" lightness comes from beaten egg whites and the small amount of flour used in them. Tortes can be white, chocolate or marble, and enriched with honey, coconut, poppy seed, walnuts, or almonds. Or make them dairy by adding cheese or decorating them with whipped cream.

Tortes can be baked in any shape: square or round using spring form or tube pans. Round cakes are easy to frost and decorate. You can also double or triple the basic amount of batter, so that the cake will be high and beautiful. Frostings can be used between layers and/or on top. Make the frostings even richer by adding shredded coconut, chocolate, fruit, and more.

Tortes and Sponge Cakes

Basic Sponge Cake

On Shabbos, alongside the cakes rich in fruit and various fillings, the simple, white sponge cake will not be overlooked. This light-colored cake, lemon or vanilla flavored, is delicate and easy to digest, even for the very young. This cake freezes well.

8 eggs, separated
1½ cups sugar
⅓ cup oil
2–3 tablespoons cognac, liqueur, or rum
½ lemon — juice and finely grated rind
1½ cups flour
2 teaspoons baking powder

In a bowl, beat the yolks with ½ cup sugar. Mix in the oil, cognac, and lemon juice and rind. In a separate bowl, beat the egg whites until stiff, gradually adding the remaining sugar. Gently fold the yolks into the beaten whites. Fold in the flour and baking powder. Be careful to maintain the airy texture of beaten egg white mixture. Another possibility is to add the flour and baking powder to the egg white mixture and combine all for a few seconds with an electric mixer.

Pour the cake batter into a round 10-inch pan. Preheat the oven to 350°F (180°C), and bake the cake for about 50 minutes. It is ready when a toothpick inserted in the center of the cake comes out clean.

Variation: Marble cake — divide the batter into two equal portions. To one part add 1–2 tablespoons fine cocoa. Mix until evenly distributed and batter is dark. Gently fold the dark batter into the light until you have a zebra-stripe effect. Baking instructions are the same as for the basic recipe.

Walnut Or Almond Torte

A light, delightful nut cake. The amount of flour is balanced by the addition of nuts, preserving the torte's lightness. Purim and other holidays welcome this cake. You can frost it, if you wish. The almond torte is considered finer than the walnut one. This cake freezes well.

12 eggs, separated

12 tablespoons sugar

2 tablespoons oil

½ lemon — juice and finely grated rind

12 tablespoons ground walnuts or almonds

1 tablespoon vanilla extract — used with walnuts, OR

    1 tablespoon almond flavoring — used with almonds

6 heaping tablespoons flour

2 teaspoons baking powder

Put egg yolks into a bowl. Beat lightly with 6 tablespoons sugar, oil, lemon juice and rind, nuts and flavoring until thoroughly mixed.

In a separate bowl, beat egg whites until stiff, gradually adding remaining sugar.

Gently combine yolk mixture into beaten whites. Using broad strokes, fold in flour and baking powder.

Line a 9x13-inch baking pan with baking parchment. Pour batter into the pan, and smooth top with a spatula. Bake in a preheated 350°F (180°C) oven for 50 minutes.

Insert a toothpick to check if done. It is ready when the toothpick comes out clean.

TORTES AND SPONGE CAKES

Stippled Walnut Torte

A large, tasty, attractive torte. Making this cake specially rich is grated chocolate and ground nuts. For special occasions you may, of course, add a decorative frosting, bits of nuts, and so on. This cake freezes well.

8 eggs, separated
1½ cups sugar
1 cup salted margarine
2 tablespoons rum or vanilla flavoring
½ cup cognac
7 ounces bittersweet chocolate, grated fine
1 cup grated walnuts
2½ cups flour
3 teaspoons baking powder

In a bowl beat egg yolks, ½ cup sugar, and margarine until mixture is light and creamy. Mix in flavorings, cognac, and grated chocolate.

In a separate bowl, while gradually adding remaining sugar, beat egg whites until firm. Gently fold beaten egg whites into egg yolk mixture; fold in the ground nuts.

Gently fold in flour and baking powder. Line a 9x13-inch baking pan with baking parchment — the paper should extend above the edges of the pan.

Pour batter into baking pan. Bake in a preheated 350⁰ F (180⁰ C) oven for about 60 minutes. Insert toothpick to check if done. When toothpick comes out clean, the cake is ready.

For elegant and easy serving, slice the cooled caked into three lengthwise strips. Cut each strip into narrow, high slices. If you wish, make the cake richer by frosting each rectangular piece separately for a lovely overall effect.

Cheese Torte

A light, delicious, basic torte. The baked cake is enhanced with a delicate, special cheese frosting. Chocolate sprinkles add a nice finishing touch. This cake freezes well.

TORTE

6 eggs, separated
1 cup sugar
1 lemon — juice and finely grated rind
¼ cup water
2 tablespoons oil
6 tablespoons flour
2 teaspoons baking powder

FROSTING

1½ pounds cream cheese (5% fat)
1½ cups sour cream
¾ cup sugar
1 package instant vanilla pudding mix

Preparing the torte: In a bowl, beat egg yolks with ½ cup sugar. Mix in the lemon, water, and oil.

☕ In a separate bowl, beat egg whites until stiff, gradually adding remaining sugar. Gently fold beaten egg whites into the yolk mixture. Using broad strokes, fold in flour and baking powder.

☕ Line a 9x13-inch pan with baking parchment. Pour batter into pan, and smooth the top with a spatula.

☕ Bake in a preheated 350°F (180°C) oven for about 50 minutes until golden. Insert a toothpick to check if done. It is ready when the toothpick comes out clean.

☕ Remove cake from oven and cool.

Preparing the frosting: In a bowl, combine cream cheese, sour cream, sugar, and pudding mix until well mixed and smooth. Spread frosting over the cake. Toss chocolate sprinkles on top as decoration.

☕ Refrigerate until served.

TORTES AND SPONGE CAKES

Almond-Topped Sponge Cake

A excellent white cake, rich in milk. After baking, cut the cake in half through the middle, so you have a top and bottom layer. Crown the cake with almonds toasted in caramel and enriched with a coffee syrup — a wonderfully enticing top. To make this cake pareve, substitute juice for milk and nondairy whip for dairy whipping cream. This cake freezes well.

CAKE

5 eggs, separated
1½ cups sugar
2 teaspoons vanilla extract
3 tablespoons oil
1¼ cups milk
2 cups self-rising flour

FILLING

1 cup whipping cream
1 cup milk
1 package instant vanilla pudding mix

TOPPING

1 cup shelled almonds
2 tablespoons sugar

SYRUP

6 tablespoons sugar
4 tablespoons unsalted margarine
3 tablespoons milk
2 tablespoons instant coffee powder

Preparing the cake: In a bowl, beat egg yolks with ½ cup of sugar. Stir in vanilla, oil, and milk.

In a separate bowl, beat egg whites until stiff, gradually adding remaining sugar. Gently fold whites into yolks. With broad strokes, fold in flour.

Lightly grease a 10-inch round pan. Pour batter into pan.

Bake in a preheated 350°F (180°C) oven for 50 minutes. Remove cake from oven, put it on a tray, and let cool.

Preparing the filling: Using an electric mixer or food processor, mix whipping cream, milk, and pudding. Beat until filling is smooth.

👨‍🍳 Separate the cake into top and bottom halves. Spread the filling on the lower half. Place top half of cake over the filling.

Preparing the topping: Blanch almonds for a few minutes in boiling water. Take out of water, and peel the skin. Break the almonds into coarse pieces, and put in a frying pan over medium heat. Stirring constantly, add the sugar, and continue to cook until a light brown caramel forms.

Preparing the syrup: Put sugar, margarine, milk, and coffee into a saucepan. Stir and bring to a boil. Pour boiling syrup over the almond caramel. Stirring, top the cake with the syrup.

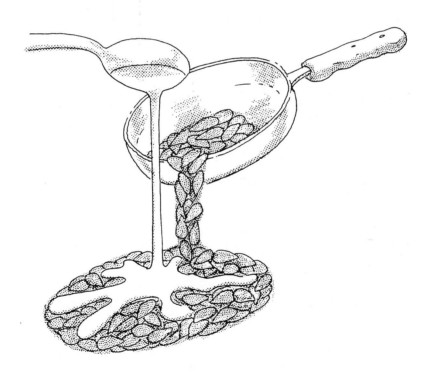

TORTES AND SPONGE CAKES

Challah Torte

Challah torte is better known by its original name of Challah Kugel. The original torte recipe called for pieces of challah soaked in wine. This recipe can be enriched with raisins, almonds, and so on. This is a wonderful way to use leftover challah in a delightful cake. This cake freezes well.

SOAKED CHALLAH MIXTURE

1 pound leftover challah or white bread

2 cups of wine

½ cup water

⅔ cup raisins — optional

TORTE

5 eggs, separated

5 tablespoons sugar

1 teaspoon vanilla

2 tablespoons oil

2 tablespoons flour

½ cup coarsely chopped walnuts or almonds — optional

½ teaspoon cinnamon — optional

1 teaspoon grated lemon rind — optional

Preparing soaked challah mixture: Cut leftover challah or bread into small pieces. Use crusts, too, to add variety. Place the pieces in a bowl, and pour wine and water over them. Add raisins. Soak the ingredients for about an hour to mingle flavors.

Preparing the torte: Put egg yolks into a bowl. Beat well with 2 tablespoons sugar, vanilla, and oil.

In a separate bowl, beat egg whites until firm, gradually adding remaining sugar. Gently stir beaten egg whites into the yolk mixture, then fold in flour. Add, optionally, nuts or cinnamon or lemon rind — or all of them. Stir the soaked challah pieces into the torte batter.

Lightly grease a 10-inch round pan. Pour in cake batter. Bake at 350°F (180°C) until the top is lightly browned.

Liqueur Sponge Cake

A light, tasty torte, the dominant flavor is the liqueur or wine. This cake is rich with nuts and chocolate. This cake freezes well.

8 eggs, separated
2 cups sugar
¾ cup oil
½ cup walnuts, finely chopped
4 ounces chocolate, finely grated
grated rind of 1 lemon
1 cup red wine or sweet liqueur
2½ cups flour
3 teaspoons baking powder

Put egg yolks into a bowl. Beat with 1 cup sugar until thick and lemony. Gently mix in oil, nuts, chocolate, lemon rind, and wine or liqueur.

In a separate bowl, beat egg whites until firm, gradually adding the remaining cup of sugar. Fold beaten egg whites into the yolks. With broad strokes, fold in flour and the baking powder until batter is smooth.

Line a 10- or 11-inch round baking pan with baking parchment. Pour batter into the pan. Bake in a preheated 350°F (180°C) oven for about 50 minutes. It is ready when a toothpick inserted in the center of the cake comes out clean.

Beautiful Spiral Torte

When serving slices of this torte, you will hear expressions of surprise — how did you make a cake with such narrow layers of cake and filling? The secret is in the assembly of the cake. You bake three cakes, and after slicing them as instructed below, you put together strips of filled cake roll over a base layer also covered with filling. The result is an elegant cake, great for serving at simchas. You can, of course, vary the colors of the cake and filling, as you please. This cake freezes well.

BASE LAYER

3 eggs, separated

3 tablespoons sugar

1 tablespoon oil

1 tablespoon cocoa powder

½ teaspoon rum flavoring

3 level tablespoons self-rising flour

CAKE ROLLS (2 ROLLS)

3 eggs, separated

3 tablespoons sugar

1 tablespoon oil

¼ lemon — juice and grated rind

3 tablespoons self-rising flour

FILLING

2 cups nondairy dessert whip

5 heaping tablespoons sugar

2 packages instant chocolate pudding mix

8 ounces bittersweet chocolate

½ cup chocolate liqueur

1 cup ground walnuts — optional

DECORATION

walnut halves

candied cherries, OR

   chocolate sprinkles

Preparing the base: In a bowl, beat egg yolks well. Add oil, cocoa, rum flavoring, and 1 tablespoon of the sugar.

🎩 In a separate bowl, beat the egg whites while gradually adding the remaining sugar. Gently combine egg whites with yolks. Using broad strokes, fold in the flour.

🎩 Line a 10-inch round baking pan with baking parchment. Pour batter into pan, and smooth the top with a spatula.

🎩 Bake in a preheated 350°F (180°C) oven for 8–10 minutes. Remove from oven and cool.

Preparing the cake rolls: In a bowl, beat yolks with 1 tablespoon sugar. Stir in oil and lemon juice and rind. In a separate bowl, beat egg whites while gradually adding remaining sugar. Gently combine beaten egg whites with yolks. Using broad strokes, fold in flour.

🎩 Cover the bottom of a 9x13-inch baking pan with baking parchment. Pour half the batter into the pan, and smooth top with a spatula.

🎩 Bake in a preheated 350°F (180°C) oven for 8–10 minutes. Remove from pan and roll up, to maintain flexibility, with a dishtowel covered with powdered sugar. Bake the second cake roll. Remove it from the pan, and roll up the same way.

🎩 Open the two rolled cakes. Cut each into four lengthwise strips, each about 3 inches wide.

Preparing the filling: Pour unbeaten nondairy whip into a mixer bowl. Begin to beat; gradually add the sugar. Continue to beat, and add chocolate pudding powder. Mix until a thick filling forms.

🎩 Break chocolate into pieces; put them in the top of a double boiler. Set over boiling water. Stir until the chocolate melts and becomes syrupy. Pour the chocolate into the pudding mixture. Continue to mix the filling while adding the liqueur. Add the ground nuts.

Assembling the cake: Put the base cake layer on a serving tray. Spread a layer of filling on it. Loosen the strips of cake roll from the baking parchment. Spread filling on each strip — a thick layer is *not* necessary. Roll up the first strip, jelly-roll fashion. Place the rolled strip in the center of the base layer, cut side down. Continue to roll up the other strips, after spreading with filling. Set each rolled strip next to the ones already on the base layer, until you have used all strips. You now have one large, beautiful spiral cake.

🎩 Spread filling on top and sides of the cake as a frosting. Draw a fork through the filling to create a decorative design.

🎩 Around the cake, alternately place walnut halves and candied cherries, or sprinkle with chocolate.

🎩 Refrigerate until serving.

Variation: Use ice cream in place of the pudding filling. Cut the ice cream into narrow layers the width of the cake roll. Frost the top of the cake with the frosting of your choice.

🎩 Freeze until serving.

TORTES AND SPONGE CAKES

Special Filled Sponge Cake

This cake is a basic white sponge cake. What makes it special is its chocolate filling and its whipped topping. When you cut the cake into slices, you have eye-catching portions of white, brown, cream, and topping. This cake freezes well.

CAKE

8 eggs, separated

1½ cups sugar

⅓ cup oil

2 tablespoons liqueur

1 teaspoon grated lemon rind

1½ cups flour

2 teaspoons baking powder

FILLING

2 tablespoons cocoa

1 tablespoon instant coffee

4 tablespoons sugar

4 tablespoons water

1 tablespoon rum flavoring or cognac

½ cup unsalted margarine, at room temperature

jam for spreading

TOPPING

NONDAIRY

1 cup unwhipped nondairy topping

about ⅓ cup sugar

1 package *pareve* instant vanilla pudding mix

DAIRY

1 cup whipping cream

1 package instant vanilla pudding mix

1 cup milk

DECORATION

½ cup unwhipped nondairy topping

candied cherries, OR

coarsely chopped nuts, OR

strawberry slices

Preparing the torte: In a bowl beat egg yolks, ½ cup sugar, oil, liqueur, and lemon rind. In a separate bowl, beat egg whites until stiff, gradually adding remaining sugar. Fold beaten whites into yolk mixture. Using broad strokes, fold in the flour and baking powder.

♟ Line an 11-inch round pan with baking parchment. Pour the cake batter into the pan, and smooth the top with a spatula.

♟ Bake at 350°F (180°C) for about one hour. Use a toothpick to check if cake is done.

♟ Remove the cake from the oven, and cool. With a knife, draw a circle around the cake, about 1 inch from the edge. Gently scoop out the inside of the cake up to the marked circle, leaving sides standing on a 1-inch high base. Put the removed part of the cake into a bowl.

Preparing the filling: Put cocoa, instant coffee, sugar, and water into a saucepan. Cook while stirring over medium heat until you have a syrup. Turn off the heat, and add rum or cognac and margarine. Continue to stir until you have a smooth filling.

♟ Using a teaspoon, drizzle some of the filling over the sides of the cake. If some drips onto the outside of the cake, it just enhances its appearance.

♟ At this stage, put the cake on a serving tray lined with a paper doily. Spread soft jam on the inside base of the cake.

♟ Pour the remaining filling over the cake crumbs in the bowl. Stir well with a wooden spoon until the crumbs have absorbed the filling. Put this mixture into the hollow of the cake. Smooth to a uniform height.

Preparing the topping:

NONDAIRY: while whipping the topping until firm, add the instant pudding and the sugar.

DAIRY: while whipping the cream, add the instant pudding and the milk. For variety, you can use mocha pudding and add a tablespoon of instant coffee powder. Gently spread the whipped topping over the chocolate layer.

Decorating the cake: Decorating this cake makes it striking. You can whip an additional ½ cup of whipped topping and make beautiful rosettes around the whipped layer or over the side of the cake that has the chocolate filling on it. You can put candied cherries and sugar into the rosettes. You can decorate the whipped topping with coarsely chopped nuts, strawberry slices, or whatever strikes your fancy. This cake is attractive and impressive.

TORTES AND SPONGE CAKES

Layered Filled Sponge Cake

These white or light-colored sponge cakes are rich with a filling of chocolate and liqueur. You can use leftover cake or one-quarter of the sponge cake to make the crumbs called for in the recipe. This cake freezes well.

SPONGE CAKE

10 eggs, separated

2 cups of sugar

¾ cup of orange juice

1 teaspoon grated lemon or orange rind

½ cup oil

2½ cups self-rising flour

½ cup liqueur

4 tablespoons jam

FILLING

1 cup sugar

1 cup water

½ cup unsalted margarine, cubed

2 tablespoons cocoa

1 generous tablespoon rum flavoring

½ cup coarsely chopped nuts — optional

⅓ cup raisins — optional

TOPPING

powdered sugar OR,

    chocolate frosting

Preparing the sponge cake: In a bowl, beat yolks with 1 cup of sugar. Stir in the juice, grated rind, and oil. In a separate bowl, beat egg whites until firm, while gradually adding remaining cup of sugar. Gently fold egg yolk mixture into beaten whites. With broad strokes, fold flour into the beaten egg mixture.

☙ Line a 9x13-inch baking pan with baking parchment. Pour cake batter into pan, smoothing top with a spatula.

☙ Bake at 350°F (180°C) for about 50 minutes. Insert a toothpick into cake to check if it is done. When toothpick comes out clean, the cake is ready.

☙ Remove cake from oven and let cool. If you are using this cake in the preparation of the filling, cut off about one-quarter of it and crumble. Put the crumbs in a bowl. Cut the remaining cake in half along the width, and place the two halves on a tray. Drizzle the liqueur over the cake and then spread it with jam.

Preparing the filling: Put the sugar, water, cubed margarine, and cocoa in a saucepan. Stir while bringing to a boil. Lower the flame, and continue to cook while stirring until you have a smooth syrup. Add the rum flavoring.

Pour the syrup over the cake crumbs in the bowl (made either from a quarter of the sponge cake or from a similar amount of leftover cake). You can add coarsely ground nuts and/or raisins to make the cake richer. Mix well into a uniform mixture.

Assembling the cake: Use a tray or baking pan with sides. Line it with baking parchment, with the paper higher than the sides. Put one half of the sponge cake into it, jam side up. Spread the filling evenly over the cake. Cover with the second half of the sponge cake, jam side down. Press the cake together well. (You can even put a heavy tray on it.)

Refrigerate for several hours, so the flavors can mingle and the layers adhere well to each other.

Adding the topping: Sprinkle powdered sugar over the cake. Instead of sugar, you can use chocolate frosting or another topping of your choice. When cake is cut, the slices are eye-catching with the dark filling between the white layers.

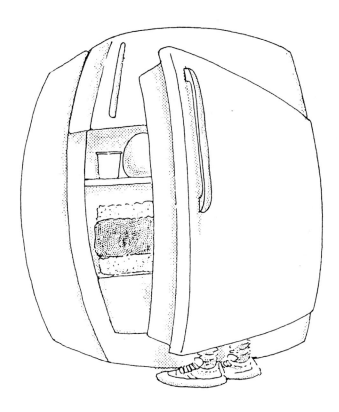

TORTES AND SPONGE CAKES

Colorful Sponge Cake, p. 101; Black Forest Cake, p. 108; Cream Cake Roll, p. 124

Orange Juice Sponge Cake

When oranges are in season, it is worthwhile making full use of them to prepare a delicious juice sponge cake. Orange frosting goes well with this cake. Freezes well.

CAKE
8 eggs, separated
1½ to 2 cups sugar (to taste)
1 cup fresh orange juice
¾ cup oil
2½ cups flour
3 teaspoons baking powder

FROSTING
½ cup unsalted margarine, cubed
2 cups powdered sugar
3 tablespoons finely grated orange rind
1 tablespoon Sabra liqueur
2 ounces grated chocolate — optional

Preparing the torte: In a bowl, beat yolks with ½ cup sugar. Beat in juice and oil.

In a separate bowl, beat egg whites until stiff, gradually adding remaining sugar. Gently fold egg whites into yolks. Fold in flour and baking powder.

Line a 10-inch round pan or a 9x11-inch rectangular pan with baking parchment. Pour batter into pan.

Bake in a preheated 350°F (180°C) oven about 45 minutes. Insert a toothpick to check if done. It is ready when the toothpick comes out clean. Remove from oven and cool.

Preparing the frosting: Put cubed margarine into a mixing bowl. While beating, add sugar, orange rind, and liqueur. Spread frosting over cooled cake. Sprinkle with grated chocolate. Refrigerate until serving.

Variations:
1) Add to the batter — before flour and baking powder — 1 cup ground walnuts and/or 4 ounces grated chocolate.

2) **For a richer cake:** Slice the cooled cake into three layers. Beat 2 cups of whipping cream with 2 tablespoons of sugar until it holds its shape. Spread 1 heaping teaspoon of orange jam over the bottom and middle layer. Spread the whipped cream over the jam. Assemble the cake. Frost the top layer. Refrigerate until served.

Fruit and Whipped Cream Sponge Cake

This exciting cake is actually a combination of two cakes. You bake it like a basic white sponge cake. Then you remove the middle, leaving only a base and thin sides as for the filled sponge cake. The rich filling is similar to that of Rich Fruit Sponge Cake. On any occasion when dairy is served, this cake is tremendously impressive, both in eye appeal and taste. This cake freezes well.

CAKE

Special Filled Sponge Cake, page 90

FILLING

1 large can of fruit cocktail
2 cups of whipping cream
2 tablespoons powdered sugar

Preparing the torte: Bake a basic white, or dark, or pink torte following the recipe for Special Filled Sponge Cake. You can vary the cake by adding 2 tablespoons cocoa or a few drops of food coloring. You can actually bake any dark cake made with a similar recipe. You can use the inner part of the cake that you remove with a spoon to make Chocolate Balls (see page 264).

♙ Place the emptied torte shell on an attractive, doily covered tray and decorate as described below.

Preparing the filling: Drain the fruit cocktail well, and put the fruit in a bowl.

♙ Beat the whipped cream until it holds its shape, gradually adding powdered sugar. Gently combine the whipped cream with the fruit. Carefully place the whipped cream mixture into the cake.

♙ You can decorate the top of the cake with chocolate flakes, nut halves, and so on. You can spread a chocolate frosting, or frosting of any other color matching the cake, on the thin sides of the cake.

♙ Refrigerate until served. On a hot day, this cake can be even more appealing when served partially frozen.

TORTES AND SPONGE CAKES

Rich Fruit Sponge Cake

A distinctive, striking cake made with no fuss and demanding no special skills. The base is a white sponge cake with interesting extra ingredients. The cake contains fruit, liqueur, and whipped cream. You can use canned fruit, such as apricots, peaches, or fruit cocktail. In season you can use fresh apricots or strawberries. This cake is particularly impressive when baked in a round pan. This cake freezes well.

CAKE

8 eggs, separated

⅓ cup oil

1 tablespoon liqueur

½ lemon — juice and finely grated rind

1½ cups sugar

1½ cups flour

3 teaspoons baking powder

FILLING AND TOPPING

¼ cup cherry brandy

½ cup syrup from canned fruits

2 cups whipped cream

2 tablespoons sugar

1 large can of fruit, OR
    3 cups fresh strawberries

Preparing the cake: Beat yolks with a fork in a wide bowl. Add oil, liqueur, lemon juice and rind, and ½ cup sugar. Mix and combine well.

In a separate bowl, beat egg whites until stiff, gradually adding remaining sugar. Gently fold yolks into beaten whites. Fold in flour and baking powder until batter is smooth.

Lightly grease or line with baking parchment an 11-inch round pan. Pour batter in. Bake in a 350°F (180°C) oven for about 55 minutes. Insert a toothpick to check if done. It is ready when the toothpick comes out clean.

Preparing the filling: Cool the cake. Line a round tray with a paper doily, and put the cake on it.

Using a long, sharp knife, cut the cake into two round layers of equal height. Place the top half on the table, cut side up. Drizzle brandy and fruit syrup onto both halves of the cake.

♀ Beat whipping cream and sugar until firm. (Be careful not to overbeat or cream will turn into butter.)

Assembling the cake: Spread half of the whipped cream over the bottom half of the cake. Place half the fruit evenly on the whipped cream, and cover with upper half of cake. Spread the remaining whipped cream over top and sides of cake. Arrange the remaining fruit attractively on the top of the cake.

♀ Refrigerate until served.

Variation: Bake the cake in a 9x13-inch pan. Spread a thin layer of jam on top. Arrange half the fruit on the jam. Prepare a package of instant vanilla pudding according to the instructions on the box. Carefully spread it over the fruit.

♀ Beat 1 cup of whipping cream with 1 tablespoon sugar until peaks hold their shape. Gently spread it over the pudding. Decorate with remaining fruit.

♀ Refrigerate until served.

TORTES AND SPONGE CAKES

Poppy Seed Sponge Cake

A tasty, easy-to-make sponge cake. Made with margarine, this cake is less light than the usual sponge cakes. You can top it with chocolate frosting. Purim is a fitting occasion for serving this torte. This cake freezes well.

7 eggs, separated
1 cup salted margarine
1½ cups sugar
¾ cup orange juice
1 lemon — juice and finely grated rind
1½ cups ground poppy seed
1½ cups flour
2 teaspoons baking powder

♕ Beat well egg yolks, margarine, and ½ cup sugar. Stir in the orange juice, lemon juice and rind, and poppy seed.

♕ In a separate bowl, beat egg whites until firm, gradually adding remaining sugar. Gently combine poppy seed mixture with beaten egg whites. Using broad strokes, fold in flour and baking powder.

♕ Pour batter into a 10-inch round baking pan lined with baking parchment or an 8x12-inch pan. Bake in a preheated 350°F (180°C) oven for about 40 minutes. Insert a toothpick to check if done. It is ready when the toothpick comes out clean.

Colorful Sponge Cake [picture on page 94]

A light, plain textured sponge cake that is divided into three colors. Each slice is attractive, impressive and delicious. This cake freezes well.

8 eggs, separated
1½ cups sugar
½ lemon — juice and finely grated rind
⅓ cup oil
1½ cups self-rising flour
2 tablespoons cocoa
up to ½ teaspoon red food coloring

ORANGE-RUM MIXTURE

½ cup orange juice
2 tablespoons rum flavoring

♕ Put egg yolks in a bowl, and beat lightly with ½ cup sugar. Add lemon and oil and stir. In a separate bowl beat egg whites until firm, gradually adding the remaining sugar. Gently stir yolk mixture into beaten egg whites. Fold flour into the mixture, using broad strokes.

♕ Divide the batter into three bowls. One of the three will remain white with a delicate lemon flavor. Sift the cocoa into the second bowl, using a finely meshed sifter. Pour red food coloring (up to ½ teaspoon) into the third bowl, and stir until you have an even, pink batter.

♕ Pour the white batter into a lightly greased 10-inch round baking pan. Gently pour the brown batter over the white. Cover the brown batter with the pink. Spread the top layer evenly with a spatula.

♕ Bake in a preheated 350°F (180°C) oven for about 50 minutes. Insert a toothpick to check if done. It is ready when the toothpick comes out clean.

♕ When the cake is baked and browned, remove it from the oven. Enrich it with an orange-rum mixture: Stir orange juice with rum flavoring in a glass. Prick the top of the cake randomly with a toothpick, and pour the mixture over the cake to make the cake softer and enhance its flavor.

TORTES AND SPONGE CAKES

Grand Coconut Torte

A coconut layer cake smothered in toppings. The base is a dark sponge layer, covered with frosting. Over that is a light, rich coconut layer, which in turn is covered with a delicate creamy pudding filling. A chocolate glaze comes on top. This large cake is wonderful at simchas. As a variation, you can use a nut sponge layer in place of the coconut. This cake freezes well.

BASE LAYER

5 eggs, separated

5 tablespoons sugar

1 tablespoon oil

4 tablespoons self-rising flour

1 tablespoon cocoa

⅓ cup wine — optional

FROSTING

1½ cups powdered sugar

2 eggs

1½ cups unsalted margarine, at room temperature

2 packages instant vanilla pudding mix

3 tablespoons water

3 tablespoons clear liqueur

COCONUT TORTE

8 eggs, separated

1¼ cups sugar

¼ cup oil

½ cup orange juice

2 tablespoons wine

1 cup flaked coconut

2 ounces grated bittersweet chocolate

1½ cups self-rising flour

GLAZE

6 ounces bittersweet chocolate

¼ cup unsalted margarine

Preparing the base: In a bowl, beat yolks, 2 tablespoons sugar, and oil. In a separate bowl, beat egg whites until stiff, gradually adding remaining sugar. Gently fold beaten whites into yolk mixture. Using broad strokes, fold in flour and cocoa. (To avoid lumps, sift them together before folding.)

☙ Line a 15x10-inch baking pan with baking parchment. Pour in batter, and smooth with spatula.

☙ Bake in a preheated 350°F (180°C) oven for about 30 minutes.

Preparing the frosting: Put sugar, eggs, margarine, and pudding into the bowl of a food process or blender. Mix until thick. Add the water and liqueur alternately. Continue to mix until frosting is smooth and velvety. Refrigerate.

Preparing the coconut layer: Put yolks into a bowl. Beat in ½ cup sugar, oil, juice, wine, coconut, and chocolate.

☙ In a separate bowl, beat egg whites until stiff, gradually adding remaining sugar. Gently fold yolk mixture into beaten whites. Using broad strokes, fold in flour.

☙ Line the same size pan (or use the same pan) as for the base layer with baking parchment. Pour in cake batter, and smooth with spatula. Bake in a preheated 350°F (180°C) oven for about 40 minutes until a brown crust forms. Insert a toothpick to check if done. It is ready when the toothpick comes out clean. Let cake cool for a few minutes.

Assembling the cake: Put the dark layer on a tray. Drizzle wine over it randomly for a richer cake. Spread half the frosting over the cake. Put torte layer over the frosting, and spread the remaining frosting on top. Freeze for 2 hours to make it easier to add the chocolate glaze.

Preparing the glaze: Break chocolate into pieces, and cube the margarine. Place both into a saucepan. Stirring constantly, melt over boiling water until a smooth chocolate syrup forms. Remove cake from freezer, and pour the hot chocolate glaze over the frozen frosting. Using a spatula, smooth it into an even layer. Let stand for a few minutes. When chocolate begins to harden, score lines on top with a knife to indicate where to cut into square pieces. At serving time, putting the slices into cupcake papers and arranging them on a tray shows them off beautifully.

☙ Refrigerate until served.

Variation: For a regular Shabbos, bake only the coconut cake, without the base layer or frosting and filling. This cake is wonderfully light.

Torte Rigo Janzi

A wonderful, dairy cake from among the best of the Hungarian kitchen. The original Hungarian name means John the Gypsy. The cake consists of two chocolate layers, vanilla frosting, and chocolate glaze. This cake freezes well.

CHOCOLATE CAKE

8 eggs, separated

¾ cup sugar

⅓ cup cocoa

1 teaspoon vanilla

½ cup self-rising flour

FROSTING

2 cups whipping cream

7 ounces baking chocolate

2 tablespoons liqueur

2 tablespoons water

CHOCOLATE GLAZE

7 ounces chocolate

2 tablespoons oil or margarine

Preparing the cake: Put yolks into a bowl, and beat with ¼ cup sugar. Mix in cocoa and vanilla.

In a separate bowl, beat egg whites until stiff, gradually adding remaining sugar. Fold beaten whites into yolk mixture. Carefully fold in flour.

Line a 9x15-inch baking pan with baking parchment. Divide the batter into two equal parts. Pour one part into the baking pan.

Bake the second portion afterwards in the same pan so that both cake layers are exactly the same size. Alternatively, pour the batter into a single, large pan and then cut the cake in half after baking.

Bake in a preheated 350°F (180°C) oven for about 15 minutes. Cool.

Preparing the frosting: Pour whipping cream into a bowl. Beat until it holds its shape. Take care to not overbeat or it will turn into butter.

Break chocolate into pieces, and put into saucepan. Pour in liquids. Melt over medium heat, stirring constantly. Let cool for a bit and then fold into the whipped cream. Put into freezer for 15 minutes.

♔ Line a tray with baking parchment. Put a cake layer on it. Lift up sides of paper higher than the cake. Cover cake with a high layer of whipped cream.

Preparing the chocolate glaze: Break chocolate into pieces, and put into saucepan. Add the oil, and put the pan into another pan containing boiling water over a high flame. Stir until chocolate melts and a smooth syrup forms. Pour the hot syrup over the second cake layer, and smooth with a spatula.

♔ Cut the glazed layer into 3x3-inch pieces. Carefully place them over the whipped cream covered layer. When serving, carefully cut pieces with a sharp, moistened knife to avoid damaging the whipped cream layer.

♔ Refrigerate until served.

Variation for cake: You can make the stages of preparation easier by simplifying the ingredients. Instead of two layers, bake a fine chocolate cake in a 9x13-inch pan. Again, we recommend lining the pan with baking parchment that extends beyond the edges of the pan.

♔ After baking, spread whipped cream frosting on top.

♔ Freeze for at least 2 hours.

♔ Make the chocolate glaze, and pour over frosted cake, gently smoothing it into an even layer.

Variation for frosting: Pour the whipping cream into a pan. Add cubed chocolate, liqueur, and water. Over low heat, bring to boil while stirring constantly until a smooth frosting forms.

♔ Refrigerate for a few hours until firm.

♔ Remove frosting from refrigerator, and put into bowl. Beat well until it holds its shape. Cover the chocolate cake with frosting. Cut carefully into pieces, and put on an attractive tray.

Variation for topping: If you want to make these chocolate slices even richer, set aside ½ cup of whipping cream. Beat it well with 1 tablespoon sugar and 1 teaspoon instant coffee.

♔ When the whipped cream is firm, put into a cake decorating tube. Make a mocha rosette on each slice, and add a chocolate-coffee bean or a candied cherry.

TORTES AND SPONGE CAKES

Chocolate Birthday Sponge Cake

A large, airy cake baked in a large sheet pan. We recommend topping this dark cake with a light, delicate frosting and drizzling a colorful glaze over it. The cake and the frosting freeze well.

CAKE

6 eggs, separated

3 cups sugar

1½ cups oil

3 teaspoons vanilla extract

1½ cups cocoa

2½ cups boiling water

½ cup wine

4½ cups flour

6 teaspoons baking powder

pinch baking soda

WHITE FROSTING

⅓ cup water

1 cup sugar

2 egg whites

2 teaspoons vanilla extract

Preparing the cake: Beat the whites until stiff, gradually adding 2 cups of sugar. In a separate bowl, beat the yolks with the remaining 1 cup sugar. Beat in the oil and vanilla.

In a small bowl, dissolve cocoa in boiling water, to prevent lumps. Stir cocoa syrup and wine into the yolk mixture. Fold the mixture into beaten egg whites. Using broad strokes, carefully fold in the flour, baking powder, and baking soda.

Line a 15x10-inch baking pan with baking parchment which extends beyond the edges of the pan. Pour the cake batter into the pan.

Bake in a preheated 350°F (180°C) oven for 60–70 minutes. Check if cake is done by inserting a toothpick. If it comes out dry, cake is ready.

Remove from oven and let cool. Decorate as you wish.

Preparing the frosting: Put water and sugar into a saucepan. Bring to a boil. Continue to cook for 7 minutes until the syrup thickens a bit.

☕ Beat the egg whites until stiff, gradually adding cooked syrup and vanilla. Refrigerate the frosting until firm enough to spread. Frost the cake.

☕ You can add food coloring to the frosting or cover it with colored sprinkles. If you wish, drizzle a chocolate glaze on top. You will have an elegant birthday cake with minimal fuss.

Classic Chocolate Sponge Cake

A rich, light chocolate cake. The frosting covering the cake is made from the cake itself. This cake freezes well.

1 cup water

1 tablespoon rum or liqueur

4 tablespoons cocoa powder

4 ounces bittersweet chocolate, broken into pieces — optional

1 ½ cups sugar

8 eggs, separated

1 cup unsalted margarine, at room temperature

1⅓ cups flour

1 teaspoon baking powder

Preparing the frosting: Put water, rum, cocoa, chocolate, and ½ cup sugar into a saucepan. Bring to boil over medium heat, stirring with a wooden spoon. Turn off heat. Beat egg yolks and add the hot syrup to them, spoon by spoon. Stir in margarine until frosting is smooth. Set aside 1 cup for frosting the cake.

Preparing the torte: In a separate bowl, beat the egg whites until stiff, gradually adding the remaining sugar. Fold the chocolate frosting into beaten egg whites. Using broad strokes, fold in flour and baking powder. Stir until thoroughly mixed. Line a 10-inch round baking pan with baking parchment. Pour in batter.

☕ Bake in preheated 350°F (180°C) oven for 40 minutes. Insert a toothpick to check if done. It is ready when the toothpick comes out clean.

☕ Remove cake from oven and pour the reserved frosting over it. Smooth with a spatula.

☕ Return the cake to oven and let it stand in it for another 15 minutes. This is a moist cake with a luscious frosting.

TORTES AND SPONGE CAKES

Black Forest Cake [picture on page 94]

Schwartzwald Torte, its Austrian name, takes a place of pride as Europe's best. The cake is rich in chocolate and almonds. Its three layers are separated by a filling that is breathtaking with rows of cherry jam, whipped cream, and candied cherries. The top of the cake is decorated with whipped cream, grated chocolate, and cherries. For best results, measure ingredients precisely and use the highest quality ingredients. This cake freezes well.

TORTE

½ cup butter, at room temperature

⅔ cup sugar

4 ounces bittersweet chocolate

5 drops vanilla extract

⅔ cup grated almonds

6 eggs, separated

1 cup flour

2 teaspoons baking powder

FILLING

12 tablespoons kirsch (clear cherry liqueur), OR
    Slivovitz (plum brandy)

3 heaping tablespoons cherry preserves (with pieces of fruit)

2 cups whipping cream

2 tablespoons powdered sugar

3 ounces pitted candied cherries

TOPPING

4 ounces bittersweet chocolate

candied cherries — optional

Preparing the torte: In a bowl, cream butter and ¼ cup sugar until light. Break chocolate into pieces, and put into a pan. Melt over boiling water. Stir into creamed butter. Add vanilla, ground almonds, and egg yolks. Mix until smooth.

In a separate bowl, beat the egg whites until stiff, gradually adding the remaining sugar. Gently fold beaten whites into chocolate mixture. Using broad strokes, fold in flour and baking powder.

Lightly flour, or line with baking parchment, a round 10-inch baking pan. Pour batter into pan.

☕ Bake in a preheated 350°F (180°C) oven for about 50 minutes. Insert a toothpick to check if done. It is ready when the toothpick comes out clean.

☕ Remove from oven and cool. To make it easier to cut the baked cake into three horizontal, round layers, freeze it for 15–20 minutes. Remove from freezer, and cut into three layers with a long, sharp knife, or pull a thread through the cake, crossing your arms as you pull.

Assembling the cake: Put first layer on an attractive, paper doily-lined tray, and begin decorating it. Drizzle 4 tablespoons liqueur over the base layer. Then spread generously with preserves.

☕ Pour the whipping cream into a bowl. Beat the cream while gradually adding powdered sugar until the cream has soft peaks and holds its shape.

☕ Gently spread a third of the whipping cream over the preserves. Place the second layer of cake over the whipped cream. Drizzle 4 tablespoons liqueur over it. Spread a third of the whipped cream over the cake layer. Sprinkle the cherries over it. Place the third layer of cake over cherries. Drizzle the remaining liqueur, and spread the last third of the whipped cream over the cake. Decorate the cake with chocolate shavings, candied cherries, or whipped cream rosettes (taken from the general amount).

☕ Refrigerate until served.

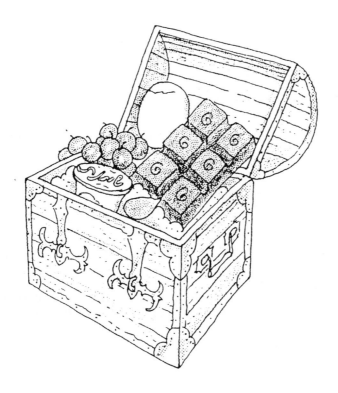

TORTES AND SPONGE CAKES

Sachertorte

Every outstanding kitchen takes pride in the Viennese chocolate torte, the Sachertorte. Home of this torte was the prestigious Sacher Hotel. After you bake the cake, you cut it into two and spread jam between the layers. A chocolate frosting covers the cake. The recipe should be followed carefully to produce the original cake. This cake freezes well.

TORTE

1 cup butter (or salted margarine)

1 cup sugar

7 ounces semisweet chocolate

7 eggs, separated

1 cup flour

1½ teaspoons baking powder

6 tablespoons high quality jam

DECORATION

5 ounces semisweet chocolate

2 tablespoons water

Preparing the torte: Beat the butter with ½ cup sugar until creamy. Break the chocolate into pieces, and melt in a double boiler over hot water. Pour the melted chocolate into the creamed butter, while stirring. Add the egg yolks and mix well.

In a separate bowl, beat the egg whites until stiff, gradually adding the remaining sugar. Gently fold the stiff egg whites into the chocolate mixture. With broad strokes, fold in the flour and baking powder.

Line a 10-inch round pan with baking parchment. Pour in the batter, and smooth the top with a spatula.

Bake for 50 minutes in a 350°F (180°C) oven. Insert a toothpick to check if done. It is ready when the toothpick comes out clean. Remove the torte from oven and let cool. Place it on an attractive serving tray.

Assembling the cake: Slice the torte horizontally into two equal layers using a long, sharp knife. Spread 3 tablespoons of jam on the top of the bottom half. Place the other half over it, and spread the remaining jam over it.

Break the chocolate into pieces, and put it together with 2 tablespoons water into the top of a double boiler. Melt it over hot water. Pour the melted chocolate over the top and sides of the cake.

Refrigerate until serving.

Marble Sponge Cake

While some people love light sponge cakes, others prefer more filling cakes like this marble sponge cake, a light cake with brown swirls. Pretty and tasty. This cake freezes well.

CAKE

8 eggs, separated

2 cups sugar

1½ cups salted margarine, at room temperature

1½ cups orange juice

rind of one orange, finely grated

5 cups flour

6 teaspoons baking powder

CHOCOLATE SYRUP

3 tablespoons cocoa

½ cup sugar

⅓ cup juice or wine

Preparing the cake: Beat the egg whites until stiff, while gradually adding 1 cup sugar. In a separate bowl, beat the margarine with the remaining sugar until creamy. Add the yolks, juice, and rind. Gently fold into the beaten egg whites. Using broad strokes, fold in the flour and baking powder.

Preparing the syrup: Stir the cocoa powder and sugar together. Pour in the liquids, and stir until syrupy.

♙ Divide the cake batter into two parts. Pour the syrup into one part, and mix well until uniformly brown.

♙ Line a 15x10-inch cake pan with baking parchment. Pour in the two mixtures, alternating between the white and the brown.

♙ Bake in a 350°F (180°C) oven for about 45 minutes. Insert a toothpick to check if done. It is ready when the toothpick comes out clean.

TORTES AND SPONGE CAKES

Simchah Sponge Cake

This tasty, reliable cake can be enriched, decorated, and matched to any joyous occasion. The cake can be white, brown, or striped. You can keep it on the simple side or on the grand, depending on the taste and imagination of the baker. The cake recommended here has vertical zebra stripes. The sides of the cake are covered with coconut flakes or ground nuts sprinkled over a chocolate frosting. The top of the cake is also frosted and decorated with light cream flowers. You can write on the cake with the frosting — use a fitting salutation, a blessing, or a biblical verse. The cake becomes even more elegant with fresh or dried fruit. Remember, this cake is good on any Shabbos, even without extra decoration. This cake freezes well.

CAKE

7 eggs, separated

2 cups sugar

⅓ cup oil

¾ cup orange juice

½ lemon — juice and finely grated rind

2 teaspoons vanilla

3 cups self-rising flour

ZEBRA STRIPES

2 tablespoons cocoa

2 heaping tablespoons sugar

3 tablespoons hot water

CHOCOLATE FROSTING

3 tablespoons cocoa

1¼ cups sugar

½ cup water

1 egg

2 tablespoons vanilla

1 cup unsalted margarine, cubed

DECORATION

1 cup coconut flakes, OR

    1 cup ground nuts

WHITE FROSTING

1 cup nondairy topping or whipping cream
1 cup milk
1 package vanilla instant pudding mix

Preparing the cake: In a bowl, beat the egg yolks with 1 cup sugar. Stir in oil, orange juice, lemon juice and rind, and vanilla. In a separate bowl, beat egg whites until stiff, gradually adding remaining sugar. Gently stir beaten whites into the yolk mixture. With broad strokes, fold in the self-rising flour.

To make the zebra stripes, stir the cocoa, sugar, and hot water in a bowl. Gently stir about a third of the cake batter into the cocoa mixture until the combination is brown.

Line an 11-inch round pan with baking parchment. Extend the edges of the paper to support the high cake. Pour the two cake batters in the following order: Using a large ladle, place white batter in the middle of the pan; using a small ladle or large spoon, put some of the brown batter over the white. Continue to add batter in the same order until all of it is used. The colors will spread in rings in the pan and become vertical zebra stripes.

Bake in a preheated 350°F (180°C) oven for about 50 minutes until lightly browned. Insert a toothpick in the center of the cake to check that it is done.

Preparing the chocolate frosting: Put cocoa, sugar, water, egg, and vanilla into a blender or food processor. Turn on the machine, and add margarine. Blend until frosting is smooth. Spread frosting on the sides of the torte. As the frosting hardens, it becomes a wonderful chocolate covering.

Decorating around the cake: Carefully lift the frosted cake, and roll it in a tray containing flaked coconut or nuts until outside is well covered with the garnish.

Line an attractive serving dish with a paper doily. Put the cake in the center of the tray. Frost the top of the torte.

Preparing the white frosting: Pour the topping for whipping (nondairy or dairy) into the processor bowl. Whip the topping while gradually adding the liquids and the instant pudding mix, until you have a light-colored, delicate frosting. Optionally, you can add sugar to the attain the sweetness you want.

Put a nozzle for making frosting flowers on a cake decorator. Fill the tube with whipped frosting, and draw small roses close together around the top of the torte. Decide what you want to write on the cake and where you will place it.

Cut a small hole in the corner of a small plastic bag. Fill the bag with the remaining frosting, and form the letters delicately on the top of the torte. You can make minor corrections using a toothpick. Decorate the cake with more flowers or fruit and so on.

Refrigerate until serving.

Twin Sponge Cakes

Two sponge cakes — a dark and a white — divided into two cakes. One cake has two white layers with a dark layer between them; the other, two dark layers and one white. Separating the layers is a luscious frosting. These cakes freeze well.

WHITE LAYERS

12 eggs, separated

2 cups sugar

1 cup water

1 lemon — juice and finely grated rind

6 tablespoons oil

2 teaspoons vanilla

3 cups flour

3 teaspoons baking powder

DARK LAYERS

12 eggs, separated

2 cups sugar

1½ cups water

¾ cup oil

¾ cup cocoa

1 tablespoon instant coffee

3 cups flour

3 teaspoons baking powder

MOCHA FROSTING

1 cup unsalted margarine, at room temperature

2 eggs

1 cup powdered sugar

2 tablespoons cocoa

2 tablespoons instant coffee

3 tablespoons liqueur or rum

Preparing the white layers: In a bowl, beat egg yolks, 1 cup sugar, water, lemon juice and rind, oil, and vanilla.

☞ In a separate bowl, beat the egg whites until stiff, gradually adding the remaining sugar. Gently fold beaten whites into yolk mixture. Using broad strokes, fold in flour and baking powder.

👨‍🍳 Line a 9x13-inch baking pan with baking parchment that extends beyond edges of the pan. Pour batter into the pan and smooth top with spatula.

👨‍🍳 Bake in a preheated 350°F (180°C) oven for about 1 hour. Insert a toothpick to check if done. It is ready when the toothpick comes out clean.

👨‍🍳 Place cake on rack to cool. When cool, cut into three round layers, using a long, serrated knife.

Preparing the dark layers: In a bowl, beat lightly egg yolks, 1 cup sugar, 1 cup water, and oil. Dissolve cocoa and instant coffee in ½ cup boiling water. Pour, while stirring, into the yolk mixture.

👨‍🍳 In a separate bowl, beat egg whites until stiff, gradually adding remaining sugar. Gently fold beaten whites into yolk mixture. With broad strokes, fold in the flour and baking powder.

👨‍🍳 Line a 9x13-inch baking pan with baking parchment that extends beyond edges of the pan. Pour batter into the pan, and smooth top with spatula.

👨‍🍳 Bake at 350°F (180°C) for about 1 hour.

👨‍🍳 When cake is cool, remove from pan and cut into three round layers with a long, serrated knife.

Preparing the frosting: Put soft margarine, cubed, into a blender or food processor. Add eggs, sugar, cocoa, instant coffee, and liqueur. Process until frosting is smooth and light. For a rich, thick topping, make a double batch. If you wish, use a different flavor frosting.

Assembling the cakes: Line two trays with baking parchment. On one tray, put a white layer; on the other, a dark layer. Frost both using a quarter of the frosting. Place a dark layer over the white layer, and a white layer over the dark. Frost with another quarter of the frosting. Place a white layer over the dark layer, and a dark layer over the white. Spread the remaining frosting over the tops and sides.

👨‍🍳 You can add a decorative touch by zigzagging through the frosting with a fork, or by sprinkling bits of nuts, chocolate shavings, candied cherries, and so on.

Variation: Instead of dark and light layers, you can bake a pink cake. Add a few drops of red food coloring to the light cake batter, or to only a third of it. You can stack the brown, white, and pink layers as you wish.

TORTES AND SPONGE CAKES

Festive 3-Layer Sponge Cake

Are you planning a special, impressive event at which you want to serve beautiful, high slices of a wonderful layer cake? This is the recipe you're looking for. You assemble this cake using three layers: light–dark–light, with a delicate combination of icings between them. The icings are enriched with walnuts, almonds, coffee, and chocolate. You can also use Lemon Cake (page 118) as a base for this cake and frost only with lemon icing. The results are great. This cake freezes well.

WHITE LAYERS (2 LAYERS)

10 eggs, separated

2 cups sugar

¼ cup orange (or lemon) juice

¼ oil

1 teaspoon vanilla

1 teaspoon baking powder

2 cups flour

DARK LAYER (1 LAYER)

5 eggs, separated

1 cup sugar

2 tablespoons orange or lemon juice

2 tablespoons oil

1 teaspoon vanilla

2 tablespoons cocoa

1 cup self-rising flour

CHOCOLATE FROSTING

1¾ cups unsalted margarine, at room temperature

1½ cups sugar

5 eggs

7 ounces baking chocolate

½ cup water

3 tablespoons instant coffee

2 cups ground nuts

ALMOND FROSTING

1½ cups shelled almonds

1 tablespoon unsalted margarine

1 cup unsalted margarine

1½ cups powdered sugar

1 teaspoon vanilla

MOCHA FROSTING

2 cups unsalted margarine, at room temperature

2 eggs

1½ cups powdered sugar

2 teaspoons vanilla

2 tablespoons instant coffee

1 tablespoon boiling water

☞ You bake this cake in stages. When the cakes are baked, you make the frostings, and then you assemble the cake.

Preparing the white layers: Put egg whites into a mixer bowl. Beat until firm, gradually adding 1 cup sugar. In a separate bowl, beat egg yolks until light with 1 cup sugar. Mix in the juice, oil, vanilla, and baking powder. Gently fold beaten whites into yolk mixture. Then, using broad strokes, fold in flour. From this batter, you will bake two layers — for the first and third layer of the assembled cake.

☞ Line two 9x13-inch baking pans with baking parchment. (If only one pan is available, bake layers in two shifts.) Pour half the batter into each pan.

☞ Bake for 15 minutes in a preheated 350°F (180°C) oven. Insert a toothpick to check if done. It is ready when the toothpick comes out clean. Carefully remove from pans by lifting with the baking parchment. Cool on rack.

Preparing the dark layer: Put yolks into a bowl. Beat until light with ½ cup sugar. Mix in juice, oil, and vanilla. In a separate bowl, beat the egg whites until stiff, gradually adding the remaining sugar. Gently fold yolk mixture into beaten whites. Sift flour and cocoa together (to prevent lumps). Using broad strokes, fold into egg mixture.

☞ Line a 9x13-inch pan with baking parchment. Pour in batter.

☞ Bake for 15 minutes in a preheated 350°F (180°C) oven. Insert a toothpick to check if done. When done, carefully remove from pan by lifting with the baking parchment. Cool on rack.

Preparing the chocolate frosting: Put softened margarine, sugar, and eggs into the container of a blender or food processor. Process thoroughly. Break chocolate into pieces, and put into a saucepan. Add water and instant coffee. Stirring constantly with a wooden spoon, melt over medium heat. Add the melted chocolate to the margarine mixture, and continue to process until frosting is smooth. Mix nuts in thoroughly.

Preparing the almond frosting: To add flavor, roast almonds in oven as follows: Put almonds into a pan with 1 tablespoon margarine. Heat oven to 375°F (190°C). Roast for 5 to 10 minutes, stirring occasionally with a wooden spoon. Remove from oven and grind.

☕ Put margarine, powdered sugar, and vanilla into the container of a blender or food processor. Process until smooth. While processor is running, add the ground almonds and mix for a few seconds.

Preparing the mocha frosting: Put margarine into food processor container. Add eggs, powdered sugar, vanilla, and instant coffee dissolved in water. Process until smooth.

Assembling the cake: Line an attractive serving tray with baking parchment cut to the size of the cake. Put the first layer on it. Spread a quarter of the chocolate frosting over it.

☕ Put cake into freezer for 10 minutes, so frosting will become firm.

☕ Remove from freezer, and spread half of the almond frosting over the chocolate. Gently spread another quarter of the chocolate frosting over it. The cake is now covered with brown, white, and brown layers of frosting.

☕ Carefully place the dark cake layer over the frosted layer. Ice in the same order as the first layer: a quarter of the chocolate frosting, half of the almond, and again a quarter of the chocolate.

☕ Place the second light layer over the frosted second layer. Spread mocha frosting over top and sides. Any leftover frosting can be frozen for future use.

☕ For easy and eye-catching serving, cut cake lengthwise into three parallel strips. Frost cut sides with mocha frosting. You will have three long, narrow cakes. Draw a fork over the frosting on the top. For topping, sprinkle chocolate sprinkles or put candied cherries in frosting rosettes, and so on.

Lemon Cake Variation: Bake the three layers, two light and one dark. Make lemon frosting, and spread it between the layers and on top of cake.

> 1⅔ cup unsalted margarine, at room temperature
> 1½ cups powdered sugar
> 2 teaspoons vanilla
> 3 egg yolks
> juice of 1½ ripe lemons

☕ Put margarine into blender. Add sugar and vanilla and blend until smooth. Add yolks and juice, continuing to blend until velvety.

☕ Refrigerate 1 hour to become firm. Frost and decorate cake.

ENTICING, mouth-watering, and striking in appearance, cake rolls are made with a thin layer of sponge cake filled with a variety of creamy fillings. Bake a white cake roll and fill it with brown or pink filling, or the opposite. Baking time is short. The crucial step is releasing the cake from the pan: spread a dishtowel on a table, sprinkle powdered sugar on the towel to prevent the cake from sticking to it. Gently turn out the hot cake onto the towel, and peel off the baking parchment that lined the baking pan. Then roll the cake with the towel to maintain the flexibility of the cake. Let the rolled cake cool for a few minutes, and then unroll it. Spread the filling on the cake and re-roll. Frost the top and decorate with nuts, chocolate shavings, or powdered sugar.

Cake Rolls

Cherry Cake Roll

This filled cake roll does not freeze well.

CAKE ROLL

4 eggs, separated
4 tablespoons sugar
2 tablespoons oil
4 tablespoons self-rising flour
½ lemon — juice and finely grated rind

FILLING

2½ cups canned cherries, chopped
1 cup dry red wine
⅓ cup sugar
1 cup of juice from the canned cherries
2 heaping tablespoons cornstarch
pinch cinnamon

DECORATION

powdered sugar

Preparing the cake roll: Beat the egg yolks well with 2 tablespoons of sugar. Stir in oil and lemon. In a separate bowl, beat the egg whites until firm, while adding the remaining sugar. Gently fold the beaten yolks into the whipped egg whites. Using broad strokes, fold the flour into the egg mixture.

♟ Line a 15x10x1-inch jelly-roll pan with baking parchment. Spread batter evenly into the pan.

♟ Bake the cake at 350°F (180°C) for 12 to 15 minutes until nicely golden.

♟ Turn cake out onto a dishtowel dusted lightly with powdered sugar. Carefully peel off the baking parchment. Roll up the towel and cake, starting at the short end. Let cool.

Preparing the filling: Drain the cherries; put a cup of the juice into a bowl. Place the fruit in a second bowl. Put the wine and sugar into a saucepan, and bring to a boil. Mix the cherry juice with the cornstarch; add the cinnamon. Pour the cornstarch mixture into the boiling wine, stir until a smooth pudding forms.

Assembling the cake: Unroll the cake, and spread the pudding mixture over it. Sprinkle the fruit over the pudding layer. Roll up the cake again. Sprinkle powdered sugar over the cake. Refrigerate until served.

Chocolate Cake Roll

Cake rolls can be varied. This one is a brown cake roll with a chocolate filling. You can, of course, use another filling to produce a different cake that will be a pleasant surprise for the family. This cake freezes well.

CAKE ROLL

4 eggs, separated

½ cup sugar

3 tablespoons lukewarm water

¾ cup self-rising flour

2 tablespoons cocoa

FILLING

3½ ounces chocolate

¾ cup unsalted margarine, cubed

1 egg yolk

1 cup confectioner's sugar

1 teaspoon instant coffee powder

Preparing the cake roll: In a bowl, beat the egg yolks, ¼ cup sugar, and water. In a separate bowl, beat the egg whites until stiff, gradually adding the remaining sugar. Fold beaten whites into yolk mixture. Sift flour and cocoa onto the batter and fold in with broad, gentle strokes.

Line a 15x10-inch cake roll pan with baking parchment. Pour batter into pan. With a spatula, spread to a layer of uniform height.

Bake in a preheated 350°F (180°C) oven for 8–10 minutes. Gently turn out the cake onto a dishtowel dusted with powdered sugar. Peel off the baking parchment. Starting from the short end, roll the cake with the towel. Let cool.

Preparing the filling: Break the chocolate into pieces. Put the chocolate and cubed margarine into a saucepan. Melt over medium heat while stirring with a wooden spoon. Turn off the heat, and continue to stir while adding the egg yolk, sugar, and instant coffee until you have a uniform chocolate filling.

Refrigerate the filling for an hour until firm.

Open the cake roll, and spread the filling over it. You can use part of the filling as a frosting. For decoration, you can use chocolate shavings, bits of nuts, or candied cherries.

Whipped Cream Cake Roll

[picture on page 94]

This recipe is actually the most basic of all cake rolls. You can add to it and make variations that change the cake into something new. In addition, this cake has a rich dairy filling made with whipped cream combined with vanilla or chocolate pudding. This cake freezes well.

CAKE ROLL

6 eggs, separated

6 tablespoons sugar

1 tablespoon oil

2 teaspoons vanilla extract

6 tablespoons flour

FILLING

1 cup whipping cream

1 package instant pudding mix — any flavor

1 cup milk

DECORATION

handful of coarsely chopped walnuts or sliced strawberries

handful of chocolate flakes

Preparing the cake roll: In a bowl, beat yolks and 2 tablespoons sugar. Beat in oil and vanilla. In a separate bowl, beat the egg whites until stiff, gradually adding the remaining sugar. Fold the yolks into the whites; then gently fold in the flour.

☕ Line a 15x10-inch pan with baking parchment. Spread the batter evenly on the pan.

☕ Bake in a preheated 350°F (180°C) oven for 10–15 minutes until lightly browned. Loosen the cake from the pan and arefully peel off the baking parchment and turn cake out onto a dishtowel dusted lightly with powdered sugar. Starting at the short end, roll up the towel and cake. Let cool.

Preparing the filling: Pour the whipping cream into a mixing bowl. Beat with an electric mixer; when the cream begins to become firm, add pudding and milk. Continue to beat until you have a smooth, uniform cream.

☕ Spread the whipped cream over the open cake roll. Roll up carefully, and place on an attractive tray. You can spread two-thirds of the whipped cream in the cake and the rest over the top. Decorate with pieces of nuts, chocolate flakes, and so on.

☕ Refrigerate until served.

Filling variation: Instead of a filling made with whipped cream and pudding, you can use whipped cream alone. Beat 1 cup of whipping cream with ½ cup powdered sugar until firm. Spread over the open cake, and then roll up.

Note: To give the whipped cream more taste, add another step to the preparation: A few hours before beating the cream, pour it into a saucepan. Add the powdered sugar, and heat it just until bubbles begin to appear around the edges of the pan — do not boil! Remove from heat and refrigerate. When assembling the cake roll, beat the whipping cream until firm, and spread it over the open cake. Roll up.

Topping variation: Break 4 ounces of chocolate into pieces. Put the chocolate in the top of a double boiler. Place over boiling water, and heat until chocolate melts. Pour the hot melted chocolate over the rolled up cake. You can decorate the top with bits of nuts or chocolate.

Strawberry Cake Roll

A delicate, white cake roll with a pink filling rich with whipped cream and sliced strawberries. Powdered sugar tops it all. This cake freezes well.

CAKE

5 eggs, separated
2 tablespoons hot water
½ cup sugar
1 teaspoon vanilla extract
½ teaspoon grated lemon rind
1¼ cups flour

FILLING

2 cups strawberries
about ½ cup sugar
1 cup whipping cream
1 package instant strawberry pudding mix
1 cup milk

DECORATION

powdered sugar

Preparing the cake roll: In a bowl, beat the yolks, water, 1 tablespoon sugar, vanilla, and lemon rind. In a separate bowl, beat the egg whites until stiff, gradually adding the remaining sugar. Fold the beaten egg whites into the yolks. Gently fold in the flour.

Line a 9x13-inch pan with baking parchment. Spread batter evenly in the pan.

Preheat oven to 350°F (180°C) and bake for 8–10 minutes until lightly browned. Loosen sides, and turn out on a dishtowel lightly dusted with powdered sugar. Starting at short end, roll cake and towel together. Let cool.

Preparing the filling: Wash and hull the berries. Crush half, and cut the other half into quarters. Add the sugar to the strawberry puree. Whip the cream, pudding, and milk together until the combination is smooth and holds its shape. Gently fold the crushed and the quartered berries into the whipped mixture.

Unroll the cake. Spread the strawberry cream evenly over the cake. Roll it up again (without the towel). Refrigerate for at least an hour.

Sprinkle with powdered sugar before serving.

Apple Cake Roll

Apple cake roll differs from other cake rolls in the way it is baked — together with the filling. After baking, it is shaped into a cake roll and sprinkled with powdered sugar. This cake freezes well.

FILLING

1½ cups coarsely chopped walnuts

5 large, tart apples, unpeeled

¾ cup sugar

1 level teaspoon cinnamon

3–4 tablespoons cake or bread crumbs

CAKE

5 eggs, separated

5 tablespoons sugar

1 tablespoon oil

¼ cup water

5 tablespoons flour

DECORATION

powdered sugar

Preparing the filling: Line a 15x10-inch baking pan with baking parchment. Sprinkle half the chopped nuts over it. Wash, dry, and grate the apples coarsely into a bowl; mix with the sugar and cinnamon.

Stir the apple mixture, and lightly squeeze to remove excess liquid. Sprinkle the apples evenly over the nuts. Sprinkle the remaining nuts over the apples. To absorb excess moisture from the apples, sprinkle crumbs over the filling.

Preparing the cake roll: Beat the egg whites until stiff, gradually adding the sugar. In a separate bowl, beat the yolks, and mix in the oil and water. Fold the yolks into the beaten whites. Gently fold in the flour. Spread the batter over the filling.

Preheat the oven to 350°F (180°C). Bake for 15-20 minutes until nicely browned. Gently turn out the cake onto a dishtowel dusted with powdered sugar. Peel off the baking parchment. Starting from the short end, roll the cake with the towel. Let cool.

Unroll the cake. Spread the cake with the apple filling and roll up. Sprinkle powdered sugar on top.

Refrigerate until served.

Apple and Apple Pudding Roll-Up

As a variation, you may fill the basic roll-up with a cooked apple mixture. Powdered sugar dusts the top of the cake roll. This cake does not freeze well.

CAKE ROLL

5 eggs, separated

5 tablespoons sugar

2 tablespoons oil

½ lemon — juice and finely grated rind

5 tablespoons flour

FILLING

1¼ pounds baking apples, peeled and cored

½ cup sugar

½ lemon — juice and finely grated rind

2 cups water

2 tablespoons cornstarch

pinch cinnamon

pinch ground cloves

pinch nutmeg

DECORATION

powdered sugar

Preparing the cake roll: In a bowl, beat the egg yolks, 2 tablespoons sugar, oil, and lemon.

☕ In a separate bowl, while gradually adding the remaining sugar, beat the egg whites until peaks are firm. Lightly fold the egg yolk mixture into the beaten egg whites. Fold in the flour.

☕ Line a 15x10-inch baking pan with baking parchment. Spread the batter in an even layer.

☕ Bake in a preheated 350°F (180°C) oven for about 15 minutes until top is golden.

☕ Gently turn out the cake onto a dishtowel dusted with powdered sugar. Peel off the baking parchment. Starting from the short end, roll the cake with the towel. Let cool.

Preparing the filling: Slice the apples into thin slices. Put the sugar, lemon, and 1 cup of water into a bowl; add the apple slices. Bring to a boil over a high flame in a covered pot. Lower flame, and cook for 15 minutes. Drain liquid into a bowl. Take 1 cup of the juice from it.

👩‍🍳 Pour the 1 cup of juice into a pan, and bring to a boil. In a bowl, thin the cornstarch with the remaining water and the spices. Pour into the boiling juice. Stir until the mixture has texture of pudding. Turn off stove. Lightly stir the pudding into the cooked apple slices.

Assembling the cake roll: Unroll the cake, spread the apple mixture on it. Roll the cake over the filling. Dust the top of the cake roll with powdered sugar.

CAKE ROLLS

CRESCENTS are known by many names, such as *"kipelach"* in Hungary and *"rugelach"* in Jerusalem. The different terms all mean crescent-shaped baked goods with rich fillings. The French, known for their croissants, prefer to bake them without a filling.

The crescents can be baked with fresh yeast, or dry yeast, puff pastry, phyllo leaves, or a rich dairy dough. The fillings, too, can be made from various ingredients, among them cocoa, cinnamon, spiced nuts, cheese, and poppy seeds. A sprinkling of powdered sugar adds a nice touch at serving time.

Crescents

Dairy Nut Crescents

From this small amount of dough you get 48 pieces of wonderful kipelach. The dairy texture of the dough becomes flaky as it bakes, and it takes on the flavor of excellent puff pastry. The dough works well for Cheese Pockets for Shavuos. These crescents freeze well.

DOUGH

2½ heaping cups flour

8 ounces cream cheese (9% fat)

1¼ cups salted margarine, cubed

1 tablespoon sugar

FILLING

1½ cups ground walnuts

⅔ cup sugar

4 tablespoons milk

finely grated rind of 1 lemon

1 teaspoon vanilla extract

⅔ cup raisins

TOPPING

1 egg, beaten

powdered sugar

Preparing the dough: Sift flour into a bowl. Add cheese, margarine and sugar. Knead into a smooth dough. Cover dough and refrigerate one hour.

Preparing the filling: Put the nuts, sugar, and milk into a dairy saucepan. Stirring constantly with a wooden spoon, cook over medium heat until thick. Remove from heat, and stir in the lemon rind and vanilla.

Making the crescents: Flour a work surface. Remove the ball of dough from the refrigerator, and divide it into six equal parts. Roll each portion out into a circle about 10 inches in diameter. Divide the circle into eight pieces. On each piece, put one teaspoon of filling, and flatten it a bit on the wider side of the dough. Add a few raisins and roll up from the outer edge inward. Tip the ends to create a crescent shape.

♕ Line two large cookie sheets with baking parchment. Place crescents on the cookie sheet, leaving a small amount of space between each. Brush with beaten egg.

♕ Preheat oven to 375°F (190°C) and bake for 15 minutes or until lightly browned. Sprinkle with powdered sugar.

Pareve Cheese-Flavor Crescents

This recipe makes 72 crescents from cold yeast dough, with no filling. They are easy to make, even for beginners. The wonderful "cheese flavor" comes from dipping them in a vanilla–lemon syrup after the baking. These crescents freeze well.

DOUGH

7½ cups flour

2 packages dry yeast

1 cup lukewarm water

2 cups salted margarine, cubed

4 eggs

6 tablespoons sugar

pinch salt

SYRUP

2 cups water

2 tablespoons vanilla extract

juice of 1 large lemon

1½ cups sugar

Preparing the dough: Sift the flour into a bowl. Dissolve the yeast in the water, and pour into a well in the flour. Add all other ingredients. Knead into a smooth, pliable dough. Flour it lightly, cover with a dishtowel, and refrigerate for 1½ hours.

Making the crescents: Lightly flour a work surface. Divide the dough into six balls. Roll each ball into a circle 12 inches across. Cut each circle into 12 wedges. Beginning at the wide edge of the wedge, roll toward the point. Bend the edges to give a crescent shape.

♟ Line a large cookie sheet with baking parchment (you will need three trays for the whole batch). Place crescents on the cookie sheet, leaving a small amount of space between each.

♟ Bake in a preheated 350°F (180°C) oven for about 35 minutes until lightly browned.

Preparing the syrup: Pour the water, vanilla, lemon juice, and sugar into a saucepan. Bring to boil. Carefully dip each baked crescent into syrup, and put on a tray to dry. These *pareve* crescents have a delicate cheese flavor.

Folded-Dough Crescents

Courtesy of Aunt Seren — This recipe makes 96 Hungarian crescents, kipelach. The dough is prepared in the manner of puff pastry, and the filling is rich in nuts or poppy seed. The effort you invest in these crescents is rewarded with a large batch of tasty pastries, especially good at Purim time or any festive event. These crescents freeze well.

DOUGH I

5 cups flour

1½ teaspoons baking powder

1 cake compressed yeast

about 1 cup juice or soda water

2 eggs

4 tablespoons sugar

DOUGH II

2 cups flour

2 cups salted margarine

FILLING

3½ cups ground walnuts

1¾ cups sugar

finely grated rind of 1 lemon

1 heaping tablespoon cinnamon — optional

12 tablespoons jam

1 egg, beaten

DECORATION

powdered sugar

Preparing Dough I: Sift the flour and baking powder into a bowl large enough for kneading. Dissolve the yeast in the juice or soda, and pour it into a well in the flour. Add eggs and sugar, and knead all into a pliable, easy-to-roll dough.

Preparing Dough II: Knead the flour and margarine into an oily, soft dough.

☙ Divide Dough I into three parts. Roll each ball into a large circle, 15 inches in diameter. Divide Dough II into three parts. Spread over each of the large circles of Dough I a part of Dough II. Fold circles of dough into an envelope, in the manner of puff pastry, by folding the edges towards the center. The shape will be a long, narrow rectangle. Fold the sides again toward the center like a book. Repeat the process with the other two circles of dough. Seal the pieces of folded dough in nylon wrap, and refrigerate for 2 hours.

♆ Liberally flour a work surface. Remove dough from the refrigerator. Cut each of the three folded doughs into two. Roll each of the six pieces of dough, and fold them again like envelopes. Refrigerate again for 2 hours.

♆ Remove from the refrigerator. Roll each piece of dough into a circle 15 inches in diameter.

Preparing the filling: In a bowl, mix ground nuts, sugar, lemon rind, and cinnamon. You can also use a poppy seed filling (see Puzhon Crescents, page 136).

Making the crescents: Spread 2 tablespoons jam evenly on each of the six circles of dough. Cut each circle into 16 wedges (first cut into quarters and then each quarter into four). Put about 1 teaspoon filling at the wide end of the wedge. Beginning at the wide end of the wedge, roll toward the point. Curve edges to shape crescents.

♆ Line two cookie trays with baking parchment. Place the crescents close together on the trays. Brush the tops with beaten egg.

♆ Bake in a preheated 375°F (190°C) oven for about 25 minutes until nicely browned.

♆ Using a fine sifter, generously sprinkle powdered sugar over the crescents.

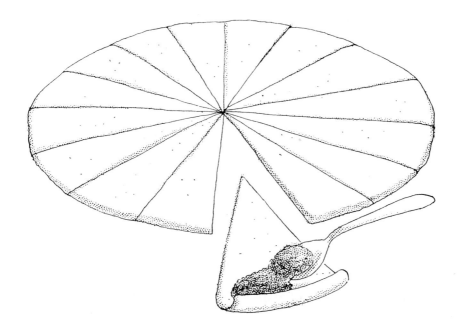

CRESCENTS

Puzhon Crescents

The story has it that these crescents originated in Pressburg (now in Slovakia). You bake 48 crescents from tasty, light. flaky dough. The filling can be a rich nut mixture or a tasty poppy seed mixture. It's good to make a double batch of dough, so you can use both fillings. These crescents freeze well.

DOUGH

4 cups flour

1½ cups salted margarine, cubed

pinch salt

½ cup sugar

½ cake compressed yeast

about ½ cup orange juice or water

finely grated rind of 1 orange — optional

3 egg yolks

NUT FILLING

4 tablespoons honey or jam

1½ cups ground walnuts

¾ cup raisins

1 cup sugar

1 tablespoon lemon rind

POPPY SEED FILLING

3 cups ground poppy seed

1½ cups sugar

2 tablespoons jam

½ cup sweet wine

finely grated rind of 1 lemon

¼ cup salted margarine

4 tablespoons jam for spreading

DECORATION

powdered sugar

Preparing the dough: Sift the flour into a wide bowl. Add cubed margarine, salt, sugar, and yeast dissolved in liquid. Add the orange rind and egg yolks. Combine all ingredients well into a pliable dough easy to roll out — the amount of liquid may have to be adjusted. Shape dough into a ball. Lightly flour a work surface.

☕ Line two large cookie trays with baking parchment. Divide the dough into four parts. Roll each part into a circle 12 inches in diameter.

Preparing the nut filling: In a bowl, mix well nuts, raisins, sugar, and lemon rind. On each circle of dough, spread 1 tablespoon honey or jam.

Preparing the poppy seed filling: Put poppy seed, sugar, jam, wine, lemon rind, and margarine into a saucepan. Cook for 8 minutes over a low flame, stirring constantly. The mixture will be soft. On each circle of dough, spread 1 tablespoon honey or jam.

Making the crescents: Cut each circle of dough into 12 wedges. Near the wide end of each wedge put about 1 tablespoon of filling. Beginning at the wide end, roll toward the point. Curve the edges for crescent shape. Place the crescents on large cookie sheets lined with baking parchment. There is no need to brush the tops with beaten egg.

☕ Bake each tray at 375°F (190°C) for about 40 minutes until nicely golden.

☕ Before serving, sprinkle crescents with powdered sugar using a fine sifter.

Chocolate Crescents

The 48 crescents (kipelach or rogelach) look like bakery goods, but their taste is even finer. Made from a delicate yeast dough, the crescents are filled with a wonderfully matching rich cocoa filling. These crescents freeze well.

DOUGH

6 cups flour
1 cake compressed yeast
½ cup lukewarm water
1 cup liquid (orange juice + water, or only water)
½ cup salted margarine
½ cup sugar
pinch salt
2 eggs

FILLING

1 cup unsalted margarine, at room temperature
2 tablespoons rum or vanilla extract
½ cup sugar
2 tablespoons cocoa

TOPPING

1 egg, beaten
powdered sugar

☕ Prepare the filling before the dough. Use a blender or food processor to make the cocoa filling. Refrigerate until filling is firm.

Preparing the filling: Put margarine into the blender or food processor. Add the other ingredients, and mix until well blended into smooth filling. Put the filling into a container, and refrigerate until you make the dough.

Preparing the dough: Sift flour into a mixing bowl. Dissolve yeast in lukewarm water. Pour the dissolved yeast into the flour. When oranges are in season, we recommend using the juice of two (if necessary, add water to make 1 cup). Add margarine, sugar, salt, and eggs. Combine into a pliable dough.

☕ Lightly flour the ball of dough, cover with a dishtowel, and let rise for about an hour in a warm spot.

Making the crescents: Lightly flour a work surface. Divide the dough into three parts. Roll each into a circle 16 inches in diameter.

Take the filling out of the refrigerator, and divide into three parts. Spread one part on the rolled-out dough. Cut the circle into 16 wedges. (First cut into quarters, and then cut each quarter into four wedges.) Beginning from the wide end, roll toward the point. Curve edges for crescent shape.

Line cookie trays with baking parchment. Place the crescents together on the trays, leaving some space between them.

Repeat with the other balls of dough.

Bake in a preheated 350°F (180°C) oven for about 30 minutes until nicely browned.

Cool the crescents, sprinkle with powdered sugar, and serve.

CRESCENTS

Butter Crescents

These 40 airy, tasty, unfilled crescents are also known as croissants. (You can make the dough dairy or pareve.) These crescents freeze well.

    5 cups flour
    1⅔ cakes compressed yeast
    1¼ cups lukewarm milk (or lukewarm water)
    3 heaping tablespoons sugar
    3 eggs
    finely grated rind of 1 lemon
    pinch salt
    1 cup butter (or butter-flavored margarine)
    powdered sugar — optional

☙ Sift flour into a large bowl. Dissolve the yeast in milk or water. Add the remaining ingredients, combine well, and knead into a pliable, smooth dough.

☙ Lightly flour the ball of dough, cover with a dishtowel, and let rise for about 2 hours.

☙ Lightly flour a work surface. Divide the dough into five parts. Roll each into a circle about 10 inches in diameter. Cut each circle into eight wedges. Beginning at the wide end of the wedge, roll toward the point. Curve edges for crescent shape.

☙ Line cookie trays with baking parchment. Place the crescents together on the trays, leaving some space between them, since they swell while baking. Let the crescents stand on the trays for about 20 minutes before baking.

☙ Bake for about 20 minutes in a preheated 350°F (180°C) oven until golden.

☙ Serve warm. You can sprinkle powdered sugar on top, if you wish.

Cinnamon Crescents

Rich Fluden dough is great for these crescents, as is the nut or poppy seed filling given for it. You can even make unfilled crescents with a touch of spice by rolling them in a mixture of cinnamon and sugar. These crescents freeze well.

DOUGH

Rich Fluden, page 232

VARIATION

⅓ cup cinnamon

2 cups sugar

☕ Prepare the dough according to instructions, and refrigerate it for two hours.

☕ Sprinkle cinnamon and sugar on a work surface. Divide the dough into four balls. Roll each into a circle 15 inches in diameter. As you work, turn the dough over so each side is covered with cinnamon sugar.

☕ Cut each circle into 12 wedges. Beginning at the wide end of the wedge, roll toward the point. Curve edges to give crescent shape.

☕ Place crescents on two cookie sheets lined with baking parchment, leaving a small amount of space between each.

☕ Bake in a preheated 350°F (180°C) oven for about 20 minutes.

RANKED AMONG the best pastries in Europe, strudels consist of very thin dough wrapped around various fillings. The original strudel recipe demanded special skill in rolling out the thinnest possible dough.

Customarily the dough is rolled on a linen cloth and then stretched by hand from underneath the dough to the utmost possible without tearing it. Of course, the dough can be simply rolled out with a rolling pin to obtain excellent results, too. Often served as a dessert fresh from the oven, apple strudel is the most famous of all, and goes well with a cup of coffee.

The Greek and Turkish version of strudel is baklava. Phyllo pastry, used instead of dough, is layered with a nut mixture filling in between. A sweet honey-based syrup is poured over all.

Strudels

Nut Strudel [picture on page 146]

Strudel-making originally demanded great skillfulness in knowing how to stretch a sheet of dough to the utmost thinness. The strudel in this recipe has dough that is light, thin, and easily prepared with a rolling pin. The dough is made of inexpensive ingredients, preparation is simple, and you finish with a bounty of baked goods — 15 narrow strudel rolls! This recipe claims a place of honor at family celebrations and the Shabbos morning kiddush. It is grand for any day that you wish to spend baking and stocking your freezer. The filling is scrumptious, a mixture of walnuts, raisins, sesame, and more — and all hidden in a browned roll-up covered in powdered sugar. This strudel freezes well.

DOUGH

8 cups flour

1½ cups salted margarine

1 cup boiling water

½ cup vegetable oil

1 tablespoon sugar

1 teaspoon salt

2 eggs

2 tablespoons vinegar

FILLING (FOR 15 STRUDELS)

4 cups ground walnuts (or peanuts)

4 cups sesame seeds

4 cups shredded coconut

3 cups raisins

3 cups cake crumbs or bread crumbs

1½ cups sugar

2 cups sweet wine

1 large lemon — juice and grated rind

jam for spreading

oil for drizzling

DECORATION

powdered sugar

Preparing the dough: Sift the flour into a large bowl. Add the other ingredients, and knead into a spongy dough easy to roll out. Continue to knead for a few more minutes. Shape the dough into a ball, cover with plastic wrap, and chill in the refrigerator for several hours.

👩‍🍳 Flour a working surface. Line three large baking pans with baking parchment. You can bake five narrow strudels in each pan, since they do not expand while baking.

👩‍🍳 Remove the dough from the refrigerator. Divide into 15 equal-sized parts as precisely as possible. Roll out the first portion as thin as possible into a rectangular shape. One side of the pastry sheet should be as long as the baking pan; the other side can be as long as you can roll it.

Preparing the filling: Place the nuts, sesame seeds, coconut, raisins, crumbs, sugar, wine, and lemon juice and rind into a wide bowl. Stir until you have a uniform mixture.

👩‍🍳 Spread the pastry sheet with three tablespoons of jam. Sprinkle two generous handfuls of the filling over the crumbs. (Keep in mind the filling will be distributed among 15 strudels!) Drizzle one tablespoon oil over the filling.

👩‍🍳 Gently fold over the edge of pastry, and roll up in jelly-roll fashion. Place the strudel roll into the baking pan, seam-side down. If you want to, you may score the top of the roll to indicate the portion sizes you will cut later.

👩‍🍳 Prepare the other strudels similarly. There is no need to brush the tops with egg. Occasionally during baking, gently brush the tops with oil.

👩‍🍳 Bake in a preheated 400°F (200°C) oven for 30 minutes, until nicely browned. Remove from oven. Before serving, sprinkle liberally with powdered sugar. The strudel, if covered, can be stored in the pantry.

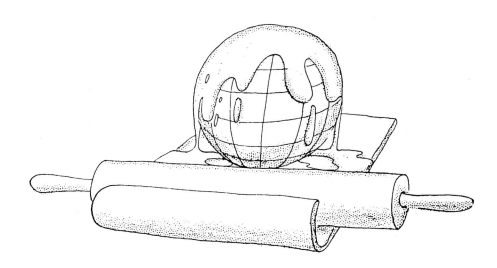

STRUDELS

Peanut Strudel, p. 149; Apple Strudel, p. 152; Nut Strudel, p. 144

Baklava

A Greek version of the European strudel. This pastry consists of four layers of puff pastry leaves rolled into thin sheets. In the middle is a sweet nut filling or one consisting of peanuts and coconut. The special eastern touch comes from the very rich, extra sweet syrup that is poured over slices of the baklava when the baking is finished. Freezes well.

DOUGH

1 pound puff pastry, ready for rolling

FILLING

1 cup sugar
3 cups walnuts, finely chopped, OR
    2½ cups peanuts, finely chopped and
    1½ cups coconut
1 heaping tablespoon grated lemon rind
1 heaping teaspoon cinnamon — optional

SYRUP

4 heaping tablespoons sugar
3 tablespoons honey
2 tablespoons lemon juice
¾ cup water

Divide the dough into four parts. Roll out four pastry sheets to fit a 7x11-inch baking pan. Grease the pan lightly and line it with the first sheet of pastry.

Preparing the filling: In a bowl, mix the sugar with the walnuts (or the peanuts and coconut), and add the lemon and cinnamon. Divide the mixture into three parts. Sprinkle one-third over the base pastry sheet, cover it with the second sheet of dough, sprinkle another third of the filling mixture over the dough. Cover this with the third sheet of pastry; sprinkle the remaining third over the sheet of pastry. Place the fourth sheet of pastry over the last filling layer.

The original recipe called for scoring the upper layer with diagonal lines. It is easier, however, to mark regular squares.

Bake in a preheated 400°F (200°C) oven for about 50 minutes until golden.

Preparing the syrup: Put the sugar, honey, lemon, and water into a saucepan. Bring to a boil. With a knife, press deeper into the scoring, and then pour the syrup over the pastry. The syrup will get absorbed into the warm cake. Before serving, place each piece of baklava into a paper cake cup.

Peanut Strudel [picture on page 146]

Rich tasting, easy-to-make cookies. You prepare them in jelly-roll fashion with a filling of peanut butter and jam, and cut them into slices before baking. This strudel freezes well.

DOUGH

8 cups flour

1½ cups salted margarine, cut into 12 cubes

2 tablespoons sugar

4 eggs

about 1 cup orange juice or water

1 tablespoon grated lemon rind

1 teaspoon vanilla

FILLING

4 cups peanuts, coarsely chopped

4 cups sugar

1 heaping tablespoon lemon rind

2 tablespoons cinnamon

12 level tablespoons soft jam

TOPPING

1 egg, beaten

powdered sugar

Preparing the dough: Sift flour into a bowl. Add margarine, sugar, eggs, juice (or water), lemon rind, and vanilla. Knead and work into dough that is easy to roll out. Shape dough into a ball, and divide it into six smaller balls.

♟ Flour a work surface. Roll each ball of dough into a sheet 12x18 inches.

Preparing the filling: In a bowl, combine peanuts, sugar, lemon, and cinnamon. Spread each pastry sheet with 2 tablespoons jam. Sprinkle one-sixth of the filling mixture over the jam on each sheet. Fold over edge, and roll up in jelly-roll fashion.

♟ Line two baking pans with baking parchment. Cut each rolled-up strudel into cookies ¾-inch wide. Pack the cookies tightly into the pan. Brush the cookies with the beaten egg.

♟ Bake in a preheated 375°F (190°C) oven for about 30 minutes. The filling may spill out a bit into the pan; it will bathe the cookies in a caramel-like sauce. When baked and lightly browned, take them out and put them on a rack to cool. Before serving, sprinkle generously with powdered sugar.

STRUDELS

Cheese Strudel

Cheese cakes also fit in well with the strudels. Rich cream cheese should be used in this recipe. This flaky cake is scrumptious and freezes well.

DOUGH
Poppy Seed Strudel Dough, facing page.

FILLING (FOR ONE ROLL)
8 ounces cream cheese
⅓ cup sugar
1 teaspoon vanilla extract
about ½ teaspoon grated lemon rind
1 egg
1 tablespoon cornstarch, OR
    1 tablespoon instant vanilla pudding mix
2 tablespoons raisins
¼ cup oil

TOPPING
powdered sugar
1 teaspoon vanilla sugar

Preparing the dough: Follow recipe instructions to prepare the dough.

☙ Line a very large baking pan with baking parchment. Flour a work surface. Divide the dough into three parts. Roll out each part of the dough into a very large rectangle — one edge the length of the baking pan, the other edge whatever results from rolling the dough until very thin. (The dough should be thin but not torn.)

Preparing the filling: In a bowl, combine cream cheese, sugar, vanilla, lemon rind, egg, cornstarch (or pudding), and raisins. Mix until well blended. Taste and adjust flavor, if necessary.

☙ Spoon the filling over the rolled-out dough. Roll up in jelly-roll fashion. Put the roll into a baking pan, and brush with oil.

☙ Bake at 400°F (200°C) for about 45 minutes until the top is browned. Occasionally during baking, brush again with oil.

☙ Before serving, sprinkle with powdered sugar and vanilla sugar. Cut into diagonal slices with a sharp, serrated knife, and serve fresh.

Poppy Seed Strudel

Next to apple strudel in popularity is poppy seed strudel. The well-oiled dough is thin and transparent. The rich filling is cooked. A festive air is added by a dusting of powdered sugar. This strudel freezes well.

DOUGH (FOR 3 LARGE ROLLS)
2¾ cups flour
1 cup margarine, cubed
1 egg
pinch salt
about ½ cup hot water
1 tablespoon vinegar

FILLING (ENOUGH FOR 1 LARGE ROLL)
2 cups ground poppy seed
⅔ cup sugar
2 tablespoons sweet wine
1 tablespoon salted margarine
1 teaspoon grated lemon rind
½ cup raisins — optional
1 baking apple, coarsely grated
⅓ cup oil

Preparing the dough: Sift flour into a bowl. Add the margarine, egg, salt, water, and vinegar. Knead into a pliable dough. If dough is too soft, add a small amount of flour. Refrigerate for about 1 hour.

♀ Line a very large baking pan with baking parchment. Flour a work surface. Divide the dough into three parts. Roll out each part of the dough into a very large rectangle — one edge the length of the baking pan, the other edge whatever results from rolling the dough until very thin. (The dough should be thin but not torn.)

Preparing the filling: Put poppy seed, sugar, wine, and margarine into a saucepan. Cook over medium heat, stirring constantly until mixture thickens. Spoon over the rolled-out dough. Sprinkle lemon rind, raisins, and grated apple on top. Drizzle oil over all. Roll up in jelly-roll fashion, and put in baking pan. Brush the top of the roll with oil.

♀ Bake for 45 minutes in a preheated 400°F (200°C) oven until lightly browned. During baking, occasionally brush again with oil.

♀ Before serving, sprinkle powdered sugar on top. Cut into diagonal slices with a sharp, serrated knife.

STRUDELS

Apple Strudel [picture on page 146]

The star among the famous strudels is apple strudel. The wrap for the filling is made of very thin pastry, whether stretched skillfully by hand in the traditional manner using a fresh linen cloth or by delicate, careful use of a rolling pin. The filling is rich with spiced apples. It can be made even more savory by adding slivers of nuts, raisins, and so on. The strudel is served fresh and warm with a sprinkle of powdered sugar. Freezes well.

DOUGH

3 cups flour

1 egg

2 tablespoons oil

2 tablespoons vinegar

about 1 cup lukewarm water

FILLING

3 pounds baking apples

½ cup sugar

1 tablespoon cinnamon

4 ounces raisins — optional

4 ounces chopped walnuts — optional

¼ cup margarine, at room temperature

½ cup bread crumbs or cake crumbs

DECORATION

powdered sugar

Preparing the dough: Sift the flour into a bowl, and add the egg — pour the oil, vinegar, and water into the mixture, and knead until dough is uniform and pliable so it may be rolled out easily. You may have to adjust the amount of water as you work.

☞ Dust a large working surface well with flour. Divide the dough into two equal parts. Roll each part into a rectangular thin sheet of pastry, one side of which should be equal to the length of a large baking pan you will use for the strudel. The other side of the rectangle is rolled out thin.

Preparing the filling: Wash and dry the apples; there is no need to peel them. Grate the apples coarsely into a bowl. Press lightly and drain the liquid from the apples. Spice the apples with the sugar and cinnamon. If you wish, add raisins and nuts. Divide the filling mixture into two.

♗ Melt the margarine, and brush it on the sheets of pastry. Sprinkle the bread crumbs over the margarine — half on each rectangle of pastry. Sprinkle the apple filling over the crumbs, one portion of filling for each sheet.

♗ Grease a large baking pan well.

♗ Roll up each pastry rectangle in jelly-roll fashion and place both in the baking pan. Brush the roll with extra oil from the pan. Gently prick the top of the strudel to allow steam to escape during the baking.

♗ Bake at 375°F (190°C) for about 45 minutes until nicely browned. From time to time as the strudel bakes, brush top with additional softened margarine.

♗ Serve with a thick dusting of powdered sugar.

STRUDELS

Apple Strudel Pudding

An apple pudding on Shabbos afternoon after cholent is a tasty, elegant course. You make the strudel on Friday, and refrigerate it. On Shabbos morning, put it over the Shabbos urn, and let it heat slowly. The pudding is studded with walnuts and raisins and has a dough reminiscent of flaky pastry — with less work. It freezes well.

DOUGH

2¼ cups flour

2 tablespoons oil

1 tablespoon sugar

pinch salt

pinch baking powder

¼ cup citrus vinegar

¾ cup water

1 cup salted margarine, at room temperature

FILLING

2 pounds baking apples

about ½ cup sugar

1 teaspoon cinnamon

handful of walnuts, coarsely chopped

⅓ cup raisins

1 teaspoon grated lemon rind

about 3 tablespoons soft jam

2 tablespoons oil

Preparing the dough: Sift flour into bowl. Add oil, sugar, salt, and baking powder. Pour in vinegar and water, and work into a soft dough.

♔ Lightly flour a work surface. Roll the dough into one large rectangle. Spread the margarine over it, and roll it up. Cut the roll into four parts. Roll each part into a rectangle, and place one sheet of dough over the other. Flour the dough well, and roll into a rectangle 10 inches by a length equal to the circumference of the round baking pan into which you will place the dough (the pan should be about 10 inches in diameter).

Preparing the filling: Wash, dry, and core apples. (It is not necessary to peel them.) Grate coarsely. Add sugar, cinnamon, walnuts, raisins, and lemon rind. Squeeze lightly, and pour off excess liquid.

♔ Spread jam on dough. Sprinkle apple mixture over jam. Drizzle the oil over the filling.

♟ Roll lengthwise as for jelly-roll.

♟ Grease a round pan well, and put in rolled dough. You can also use a rectangular pan. Cut roll into two or three parts to fit the pan.

♟ Bake in a preheated 450°F (220°C) oven for 30 minutes until nicely browned.

♟ You can serve immediately as a side dish with a main course of meat or sliced as a dessert with a cup of coffee.

STRUDELS

THE PASTRIES in this section are single-serving cakes, larger than cookies. These include light, enticing jelly doughnuts; cream- and fruit-filled sponge cakes; delicious hamentashen; cream puffs filled with whipped cream or pudding; individual cakes filled with cream and dipped in chocolate. The extra effort you take in making these baked goods is well rewarded when they grace your table in their elegance.

Doughnuts and Dumplings: a Miscellany

Yeast-Dough Hamentashen

This recipe yields a large, delectable batch of hamentashen made from yeast dough, filled with a date-nut filling. These hamentashen freeze well.

DOUGH
8 cups flour
2 packages dry yeast
about 2 cups lukewarm water
¾ cup sugar
pinch salt
2 eggs
grated rind of 1 lemon
¾ cup salted margarine

FILLING
jam for spreading
8 ounces date spread
½ cup coarsely chopped nuts
grated rind of 1 lemon

TOPPING
1 egg, beaten
powdered sugar

Preparing the dough: Sift the flour into a bowl. In a small bowl, dissolve the yeast in the water with a pinch of sugar. Let stand for about 10 minutes. Make a well in the flour, and pour the dissolved yeast into it. Add the remaining sugar and the salt, the eggs, lemon rind, and margarine. Knead all ingredients into soft dough that no longer clings to the sides of the bowl. Shape the dough into a ball; cover it with a dishtowel, and let it rise for about 90 minutes.

♔ Flour a work surface, and roll the dough into a sheet about ¼-inch thick. Cut rounds of dough with the edge of a drinking glass or cookie cutter. Gather remnants, roll them again, and cut them into rounds.

Making the hamentashen: Spread each round with jam. In a bowl, mix date spread, chopped nuts, and lemon rind. Place a small amount in the center of each round. Shape by picking up sides and pinching them together to form a triangle.

♔ Line four trays with baking parchment. Put the hamentashen on the trays, and brush the tops with beaten egg. Let rise for 20 minutes.

♔ Bake in a preheated oven at 350°F (180°C) for about 25 minutes until nicely browned. Sift powdered sugar over all.

Flaky Pastry Hamentashen

Wonderful hamentashen made with flaky pastry and traditional poppy seed filling. You can use date filling instead, of course. The hamentashen freeze well.

DOUGH

2½ cups flour

⅓ cup sugar

1 cup salted margarine, cubed

1 egg

scant ¼ cup orange juice or water

FILLING

1½ cups poppy seed

5 tablespoons sugar

1 tablespoon salted margarine

grated rind of 1 lemon

about ½ cup wine or water

⅓ cup raisins

jam for spreading

TOPPING

1 egg, beaten

powdered sugar

Preparing the dough: Sift the flour into a bowl. Add the sugar, cubed margarine, and egg. Knead into pliable dough, adding liquids as necessary. Shape the dough into a ball, and refrigerate, covered, for 30 minutes.

☙ Lightly flour a work surface. Roll the dough out to a thickness of ⅛-inch. Cut out rounds with the edge of a drinking glass or a cookie cutter.

Preparing the filling: In a saucepan, mix the poppy seed, sugar, margarine, lemon rind, and wine. Bring to a boil, stirring constantly. If necessary, add some cake crumbs to thicken the mixture.

Making the hamentashen: Spread a small amount of jam on each round. Put a small amount of the poppy seed filling and a few raisins on the dough. Pick up three sides of the dough, and pinch ends together, forming a triangle.

☙ Put the hamentashen on cookie trays lined with baking parchment. Brush the tops with beaten egg.

☙ Bake in a preheated oven at 350°F (180°C) for about 20 minutes until nicely browned. Before serving, sift powdered sugar over all.

A MISCELLANY

Bagels

A popular, tasty, easy Jewish treat. First the yeast dough rises, then it is formed into bagel rounds, boiled, and finally baked. You can sprinkle them with coarse salt, poppy seeds, sesame seeds, or rye seeds. These bagels freeze well.

DOUGH

1 package yeast

1½ to 2 cups lukewarm water

1 tablespoon sugar

4 cups flour

1 egg

2 tablespoons oil

1 tablespoon salt

TOPPING

1 egg, beaten

whole poppy seeds, sesame seeds, or rye seeds, OR
    coarse salt

Preparing the dough: Put the yeast in a cup, add ½ cup lukewarm water (from the total) and the sugar. Let stand for 10 minutes.

☙ Sift the flour into a bowl, and make a well in its center. Pour the dissolved yeast into the well. Add the remaining water (you may need to adjust the amount as you knead the dough), the egg, oil, and salt. Knead until you have a pliable dough that no longer clings to the sides of the bowl. Shape into a ball.

☙ Lightly flour the ball of dough. Cover it with a dishtowel, and let rise for about 90 minutes.

Making the bagels: On a lightly floured surface, divide the dough into 20 pieces. Roll each piece of dough between your hands into a strip about 8 inches long. Pinch ends together to form a ring. Let the rounds rise another 20 minutes on a floured surface until doubled in size.

☙ Boil water in a pot. Put in four bagels at a time and boil for 2 minutes, turning them over once. Remove from water, and place on a tray to dry while you finish boiling all the dough rings. Put the bagels on a cookie sheet lined with baking parchment, brush the tops with beaten egg, and sprinkle with the poppy, sesame, or rye seeds.

☙ Bake in a preheated oven at 400°F (200°C) for about 20 minutes until lightly browned. The bagels will have a hard, tasty crust.

Fruit Filled Baked Crepes

Sponge cake batter can be baked in various ways. One of them is to bake small "blintz" rounds, fold them in half, and fill them as you choose. A lovely filling is fruit-studded whipped cream. Among others, you can use pieces of mandarin oranges or slices of kiwi or strawberries. You serve each person an individual portion, sprinkled with powdered sugar. These crepes freeze well.

BATTER

5 eggs, separated
2 tablespoons hot water
½ cup sugar
1 teaspoon vanilla
½ teaspoon grated lemon rind
scant ⅔ cup flour mixed with
2 tablespoons cornstarch

FILLING

pieces of fresh or canned fruit
juice of 1 lemon
4 tablespoons soft jam
1½ cups whipping cream
1 package instant vanilla pudding mix
1 cup cold milk

Preparing the crepes: Into a bowl, stir the egg yolks, water, 1 tablespoon sugar, vanilla, and lemon juice. In a separate bowl, beat the egg whites until stiff, gradually adding the remaining sugar. Gently fold the beaten egg whites into the yolk mixture. With broad strokes, fold in the flour and cornstarch.

♀ Line a cookie sheet with baking parchment. Draw circles with a 4-inch diameter. On each circle, spread two tablespoons of the batter that will bake into a crepe ¼-inch high.

♀ Bake the crepes in a preheated oven at 375°F (190°C) for 5 minutes until golden.

Assembling the crepes: Mix together the jam and lemon juice. Peel the baking parchment off the crepes. Spread the jam on their bottom side. Fold each crepe in half.

♀ Whip together the whipping cream, vanilla pudding mix, and milk until firm. Fill the crepes with the whipped mixture and pieces of fruit. Serve as individual portions, dusted with powdered sugar.

Doughnuts (Sufganiyot)

Jelly doughnuts can be made from yeast dough or from baking powder batter. The best and lightest come from yeast dough that was allowed to rise well — even better, two times. The dough can be pareve, nondairy, made from water and margarine, or dairy, made from milk and butter. You can even leave out the eggs and still make jelly doughnuts with great texture. The alcohol in the dough works to prevent the absorption of oil during frying. As variations, you can use jam, pudding, or fruit preparations. You can top them with plain powdered sugar or flavored with lemon juice, fruit syrup, and so on. You can use a chocolate or caramel glaze — whatever pleases your crowd. The doughnuts can be shaped like round balls or regular doughnuts. They can also be baked instead of fried, coming out as great rolls. The amounts listed here yield 48 doughnuts. They freeze well.

DOUGH

8 cups flour

2 packages yeast

scant 2 cups water (or milk)

½ cup sugar

½ cup oil (or ½ cup butter)

1 teaspoon vanilla

1 tablespoon alcohol

½ teaspoon salt

2 ounces chocolate, melted — optional

2 ounces raisins or candied orange peel — optional

1 teaspoon grated orange or lemon rind — optional

oil for frying

FILLING

jam, OR 1 package instant vanilla pudding, prepared

TOPPINGS

a. powdered sugar, sprinkled through a sifter

b. 1 cup powdered sugar mixed with
   2 tablespoons water and
   1 teaspoon vanilla

c. 1 cup powdered sugar mixed with
   1 tablespoon raspberry syrup and
   1 tablespoon water

    d. 4 ounces melted chocolate

       2 tablespoons margarine or butter

       handful of chopped nuts — optional

    e. ½ cup sugar dissolved in 1 teaspoon water

Preparing the doughnuts: Sift the flour into a bowl. In a separate, small bowl combine the yeast and 1 cup water. Let stand for 10 minutes. Pour the dissolved yeast into the flour along with the remaining water. Add all other ingredients for the dough, and knead into soft, pliable dough that pulls away from the sides of the bowl.

☞ You can make brown doughnuts by adding chocolate, or fruit-flavored doughnuts by adding a small amount of pureed dried or candied fruit, or grated rind.

☞ Shape the dough into a ball, dust it lightly with flour, and cover it with a dishtowel. Let it rise in a warm spot until doubled in size. For added lightness, punch it down and let rise a second time.

☞ Flour a work surface. Roll out the dough to a thickness of 1 inch. Cut circles with the edge of a drinking glass or a round cookie cutter, and let rise for 20 minutes. Another possibility is to divide the dough into small pieces, shaping each into a ball; let them rise a second time on a greased cookie sheet.

☞ FOR DOUGHNUTS WITH HOLES: With a small round cookie cutter or glass, cut out a hole from the center of each ball of dough. Collect the remnants, and roll them out again.

☞ Heat 2 inches of oil in a large, flat pot. Add slices of carrot to the oil to keep it clear. When the oil is boiling, lower the flame a bit, and slide the doughnuts into the oil. Brown on both sides. Remove from the oil, and drain on paper towels.

Preparing the filling:

JAM FILLING: Fill a decorating tube with jam, and squirt it into the doughnuts.

PUDDING FILLING: Prepare the pudding according to the package instructions. Cut the doughnuts in half, fill with the pudding, and sprinkle with powdered sugar.

Preparing the topping: It is easiest to sift powdered sugar over the doughnuts.

☞ You can mix powdered sugar with vanilla flavoring and spread it on the doughnuts, or make a pink glaze by adding raspberry syrup to the sugar and vanilla.

☞ You can top the doughnuts with a chocolate glaze. Melt chocolate and margarine in a saucepan, mix, and immediately pour over the doughnuts. You can sprinkle chopped nuts over the glaze. This variation serves well as a dessert.

☞ Alternatively, you can top the doughnuts with a sugar glaze. Dissolve the sugar in water while stirring in a saucepan over medium heat. When the syrup is lightly browned, pour it immediately over the doughnuts. Serve doughnuts when fresh.

Note: The oil left in the pot after frying can be strained when cool. You can use this oil to fry another batch of tasty doughnuts.

Jelly Doughnuts

An easy-to-make recipe with an excellent, large yield. With the edge of a regular glass, you can cut out about 40 light, airy doughnuts. These doughnuts freeze well. They can be reheated before serving.

    1¼ ounces fresh yeast
    2 cups lukewarm water
    ½ cup sugar
    6 cups flour
    2 eggs
    ½ cup salted margarine
    1 teaspoon grated lemon rind
    1 tablespoon cognac

    oil for deep frying
    jelly for filling
    powdered sugar for decoration

Dissolve the yeast in 1 cup lukewarm water and 1 tablespoon sugar (taken from the total). Let stand for 10 minutes. Sift the flour into a bowl. Make a well in the flour, and pour in dissolved yeast. Add the remaining water and sugar, eggs, margarine, lemon rind, and cognac. Knead into soft dough. Shape the dough into a ball, flour it lightly, and let rise for about 90 minutes.

Flour a work surface well. Roll out dough ¾-inch thick. Cut out rounds of dough with a cookie cutter or drinking glass. Lightly grease the tops of the doughnuts, and let rise for another 20 minutes.

Put 2 inches of oil into a saucepan and heat to medium heat. Place the doughnuts in the pan, without crowding them. While frying the first side, cover the pan. When the doughnuts are lightly browned, remove the cover and turn them over. When the doughnuts are plump and well-browned, remove them from oil with a slotted spoon and drain on paper towels. It is best to keep the oil heated evenly — if it gets too hot, the doughnuts will be browned outside and raw on the inside.

You can put the jelly in the doughnuts using a cake decorating tube with a long nozzle. You can also make an indentation with a teaspoon and put in a small amount of jelly.

Before serving, sprinkle generously with powdered sugar.

American Rolls

This recipe gives you 18 super-tasty, no-fuss rolls. You make the dough with an electric mixer and drop it onto the baking tray with a tablespoon. You can eat the rolls plain or cut them in two and add a sweet spread between the halves. The rolls can be pareve or dairy. These rolls freeze well.

DOUGH

½ cup salted margarine or butter
1 teaspoon vanilla extract
1 cup sugar
3 eggs
finely grated rind of ½ lemon
pinch salt
4 cups flour
3 teaspoon baking powder
1 cup water or milk
1 teaspoon rum flavoring

SWEET SPREAD

2½ cups powdered sugar
about 3 tablespoons boiling water
2 tablespoons cocoa

Preparing the dough: Put margarine, vanilla, and sugar into a large bowl. Begin to beat with an electric mixer, and add eggs, lemon rind, and salt. When the batter is smooth and soft, beat in the flour, baking powder, water or milk, and rum flavoring.

Preparing the rolls: Line two cookie sheets with baking parchment. Using 2 tablespoons, drop dough for nine rolls on each tray, leaving space between them. Shape the dough into round mounds.

♙ Preheat the oven to 400°F (200°C). Bake the rolls for about 20 minutes until golden.

♙ Cut each roll in half widthwise.

Preparing the sweet spread: Put the powdered sugar and boiling water into a bowl and beat well. Divide into two parts. Leave one half white. Add cocoa to the other half, and beat until uniformly brown.

♙ Spread the white mixture on half the rolls, and the brown mixture on the other half. Serve fresh.

Cream Puffs

Cream puffs are made from choux paste and baked as large round rolls. After baking, you fill them with a sweet cream filling or a pareve cooked pudding. A dusting of powdered sugar decorates their tops. Another possibility is to serve them as the first course at dinner, filled with a savory filling such as tuna salad and covered with hot gravy. The puff shells freeze well. The cream fillings freeze well, but the pudding filling does not.

DOUGH

1 cup water

¼ cup salted margarine

pinch salt

1 teaspoon vanilla extract

1 cup flour

4 eggs

FILLING

VANILLA WHIPPED CREAM

1 cup whipping cream

1 package instant vanilla pudding mix

¾ cup milk

MOCHA WHIPPED CREAM

1 cup whipping cream

1 tablespoon sugar

1 teaspoon instant coffee powder

1 teaspoon boiling water

1 teaspoon vanilla extract

PAREVE PUDDING

3 eggs, separated

¾ cup sugar

2 cups water

4 heaping tablespoons flour

½ lemon — juice and grated rind

2 teaspoon vanilla extract

TOPPING

2 tablespoons powdered sugar

1 tablespoon cocoa — optional

Preparing the dough (for 10–15 puffs): Pour the water into a saucepan, and add the margarine, salt, and vanilla. Bring to boil, and melt the margarine. Remove the pan from the heat, and fold in flour, using a wooden spoon.

☞ Return the pan to the heat, and continue to stir until mixture forms a ball. Turn off heat, and remove pan from stove. Beat in the eggs, one at time.

Preparing the puff shells: Use 2 tablespoons to shape small balls or oval mounds of dough. Alternatively, use a ruffled-edged pastry tube to form the shells. A large puff shell is 2½ by 4 inches. You can make them smaller, if you wish. Skilled bakers also shape the shells as mini-swans by adding to the basic shell an additional strip of S-shaped dough squeezed through a pastry tube. Each section is baked separately and the mini-swans are assembled after baking.

☞ Line a large cookie sheet with baking parchment. Place the puff shell dough on the tray. Leave space between each shell.

☞ Preheat the oven to 450°F (220°C), and bake for 30–40 minutes until lightly browned.

☞ When baked, put the shells on a rack. Cut in half along the width, and open a bit to let out steam and prevent moisture. Fill the puff with the filling of your choice.

Preparing the filling:
VANILLA-FLAVORED WHIPPED CREAM: In a dairy mixing bowl, put the whipping cream, pudding, and milk. Beat until a smooth cream forms.

MOCHA-FLAVORED WHIPPED CREAM: Pour the whipping cream into a mixing bowl. Add sugar, vanilla, and instant coffee dissolved in water. Beat until smooth.

PUDDING FILLING: (enough for a double batch) In a bowl (or food processor), beat yolks, sugar, ½ cup water, and flour into a smooth, well-blended mixture. In a saucepan, bring to boil 2 cups water, lemon juice and rind, and vanilla. Add the yolk mixture to the boiling water, and beat until the pudding thickens and bubbles. Remove from the stove. In a separate bowl, beat the egg whites until peaks hold their shape. Gently fold the beaten egg whites into the hot pudding. Taste and adjust flavor, if necessary. Cool the pudding in the freezer for 20 minutes until quite firm. (You can make this pudding also without separating the eggs — just beat them well with the mixture of water and flour.)

Filling the puffs: Using the cream or pudding of your choice, generously fill each shell. Close the puff shell lightly in order to not crush the filling. Dust the top with powdered sugar. You can add a bit of cocoa to the powdered sugar. We recommend using a fine sifter to spread the powdered sugar. Refrigerate the cream puffs until served.

Variation: Put a chocolate glaze on each cream puff. Make the glaze by melting 4 ounces of bittersweet chocolate in the top of a double boiler over boiling water; add 1 tablespoon boiling water and 2 tablespoons unsalted margarine.

☞ Stir until glaze is smooth. Pour it over the upper halves of the filled cream puffs. Best served the same day.

A MISCELLANY

Great Sandwich Cookies

Large cookies that have a white torte layer covered with cocoa frosting, a layer of whipped filling, and a dark torte layer on top. The final touch comes with dipping the cookie into chocolate syrup. You can, of course, use different colored layers and other flavors for the frosting or filling. These cookies freeze well.

THE WHITE LAYER

6 eggs, separated

6 tablespoons sugar

1 tablespoon oil

about ¼ teaspoon grated lemon rind

6 tablespoons self-rising flour

THE DARK LAYER

6 eggs, separated

6 tablespoons sugar

1 tablespoon oil

1 tablespoon cocoa

5 tablespoons self-rising flour

COCOA FROSTING

3 tablespoons cocoa

1 teaspoon instant coffee powder

¾ cup sugar

⅓ cup water

½ cup unsalted margarine

WHIPPED FILLING

1 cup nondairy dessert whip (unwhipped)

1 package vanilla- or chocolate-flavored instant pudding mix

CHOCOLATE GLAZE

7 ounces chocolate

3 tablespoons water

⅓ cup unsalted margarine

Preparing the white layer: In a bowl, beat the egg yolks well with 2 tablespoons sugar, oil, and lemon rind. In a separate bowl, beat the egg whites until stiff, gradually adding the remaining sugar. Fold the beaten whites into the yolk mixture. Using broad strokes, fold in the flour.

☞ Line a 9x13-inch baking pan with baking parchment. Pour in the batter, smoothing the top with a spatula.

☞ Preheat oven to 350°F (180°C) and bake for about 15 minutes. Remove from oven, and cool pan on a rack.

Preparing the dark layer: In a bowl, beat the egg yolks well with 2 tablespoons sugar. Stir in oil and cocoa, and beat thoroughly, making sure no lumps remain. In a separate bowl, beat the egg whites until stiff, gradually adding the remaining sugar. Fold the beaten whites into the yolk mixture. Using broad strokes, fold in the flour.

☞ Line a 9x13-inch baking pan with baking parchment. Pour in the batter.

☞ Preheat oven to 350°F (180°C) and bake about 15 minutes. Remember, you can use other colors for the layers.

Preparing the cocoa frosting: Put cocoa, coffee, sugar, and water into a saucepan. Stir over medium heat until a smooth syrup forms. Remove from heat, and put in the margarine, stirring until it melts. Put in freezer for 15 minutes to become firm.

Preparing the whipped filling: Pour the unwhipped nondairy dessert topping into a mixer bowl. Begin to beat, and add the pudding powder. Continue to beat until a light, delicate whipped pudding forms.

Assembling the cookies: From the white layer, cut out rounds 1 to 1½ inches in diameter. Put the rounds on a tray. Spread chocolate frosting over each. Cover with whipped topping. Cut the same number of rounds, the same size, from the dark layer. Put one dark round over each frosted white round.

☞ Freeze the sandwich cookies for a few hours.

☞ Dip each cookie into the glaze, covering everything but the bottom.

☞ Refrigerate the sandwich cookies until serving.

Preparing the chocolate glaze: Make this only when the cookie layers and the fillings have been assembled and are in the freezer, because the glaze hardens quickly.

☞ Break the chocolate into pieces, and put into a saucepan. Add water and margarine. Melt over medium heat, stirring constantly with a wooden spoon.

Flaky Apple Roll-Ups

Apple roll-ups are made from a wonderful, non-oily puff pastry. They originated in Bulgaria. The filling can be a fruit mixture, a cheese mixture, or even a meat one to be used as the first course at a festive meal. These roll-ups are wonderfully flaky and highly recommended. Fruit roll-ups look great when served with powdered sugar sprinkled on top. Roll-ups freeze well.

DOUGH

3 cups flour

1 cup water

3 tablespoons vinegar

2 tablespoons oil

½ cup salted margarine, at room temperature

FILLING

2 pounds baking apples

1 cup sugar

1 teaspoon cinnamon

1 teaspoon grated lemon rind — optional

6 tablespoons bread crumbs

Preparing the dough: Sift flour into a bowl. Pour water, vinegar, and oil. Combine ingredients into a soft dough, easy to roll out. Divide the dough into two. Liberally flour a work surface; keep additional flour ready to add as you work with the dough. Roll each part of the dough into a 12-inch square. Spread a quarter of the margarine on each square. Fold each square into an envelope, by bringing each corner to the center. Now, again bring two adjoining corners to the center. Then form the folded dough into a roll. Flour the two rolls well, and refrigerate for about 3 hours.

☞ Put the rolls on a floured work surface, and roll again into squares, spread with margarine, and fold up like the first time. Flour and refrigerate for about 8 hours.

Preparing the filling: Wash, dry, and core the apples. Grate coarsely. Mix the grated apples with sugar, cinnamon, and lemon rind. You can add raisins and walnuts, if you wish. Squeeze lightly, and pour off excess liquid.

Assembling the roll-ups: Remove the rolls from the refrigerator. Cut each roll into three sections. Roll each piece into a long, narrow rectangle, 4x16 inches.

♟ Spread 2 tablespoons of filling along one short edge and sprinkle bread crumbs over it. Cover the filling by rolling the dough over twice. Cut off that section of the rectangle. You will have a long, narrow roll. Cut it in half for two individual portions. Continue in this manner until you have used all the dough.

♟ Each rectangle will yield three rolls. After cutting each into two, you will have six roll-ups from each rectangle and 36 servings from the recipe.

♟ Line cookie sheets with baking parchment. Place the roll-ups close together on the trays.

♟ Bake at 400°F (200°C) for about 20 minutes until lightly browned. Serve fresh.

♟ You can also prepare these and freeze them for baking at a later time.

Apple Dumplings

A wonderful apple cake in individual portions. Each apple is filled with a rich mixture and hidden by a wrap of flaky dough. Great as a dessert, these dumplings can also be served to guests as a special treat matched with a scoop of ice cream. These dumplings freeze well.

DOUGH

3 cups flour
1 cup salted margarine, cubed
pinch salt
about ½ cup water

FILLING

8 baking apples
½ cup bread or cake crumbs
1 tablespoon salted margarine
⅓ cup sugar
1 tablespoon cinnamon
⅓ cup raisins

TOPPING

1 egg, beaten
powdered sugar

Preparing the dough: Sift flour into a bowl. Add the cubed margarine. Cut into coarse crumbs. Add the salt and water. Knead into a soft dough, easy to roll out.

♀ Lightly flour a work surface. Roll dough into a rectangle 10x20 inches. Cut into eight squares 5x5 inches.

Preparing the filling: Wash, dry, and core the apples, keeping them whole.

♀ Put crumbs into a pan, and fry until golden in margarine. Put the crumbs into a bowl. Add sugar, cinnamon, and raisins. Mix well.

Assembling the dumplings: Fill the center of each apple with the crumb mixture. Put each apple in the middle of a 5x5-inch square, and wrap the apple in dough. Use a toothpick to keep the edges together.

♀ Put the apples in a lightly greased baking pan. Brush the dough with beaten egg. Bake at 375°F (190°C) for about 40 minutes until crust is golden.

♀ Sprinkle with powdered sugar and serve warm.

ALL YEAR LONG you can bake cakes with fruit, taking advantage of seasonal bounty. Cakes featuring fruit are light, eye-catching, and tasty. You can bake them on a bed of flaky pastry and top with a jellied layer, with whipped cream, or other delights. You can tuck the fruit filling between two layers of flaky pastry or use the fruit with a sponge cake. Cakes containing fruit are at their tastiest when fresh from the oven. If the fruits have been cooked or preserved, the cakes can be frozen. Not all fresh fruits lend themselves successfully to freezing. Each recipe provides proper storage information.

Cakes with Fruit

English Cake [picture on page 182]

A light cake, called "English cake" in Israel. This cake, enriched with raisins and candied fruit, is served cut into high, thin slices. In place of raisins, you can use bits of nuts. This cake freezes well.

¾ cup raisins (can be a mix of dark and light)

¾ cup candied fruit

3 teaspoons rum flavoring or wine

1 cup salted margarine, at room temperature

1 cup sugar

4 eggs

pinch of salt

3⅔ cups flour

3 teaspoons baking powder

In a bowl, soak raisins and fruits with the rum or wine for 20 minutes.

Beat margarine with sugar. Stir in eggs and salt.

Mix flour with baking powder. Stir into the egg mixture, and beat well until batter is soft and even. Stir in the soaked fruit, mixing well.

Grease a long, narrow baking pan (9x5 inches). Pour batter into pan and smooth top evenly.

Bake in preheated 350°F (180°C) oven for an hour, until the top of cake is crisp and lightly browned. Check if cake is done by inserting a toothpick. When the toothpick comes out clean, the cake is ready.

Peach Cake

When peaches are plentiful and quick to become overripe, the time is right to use them in baking. For this light and crispy cake, the baking pan is lined with pieces of fruit, and then the batter is poured over them. This can be served for dessert right from the oven, or rewarmed as a pudding-like dessert. This cake freezes well.

FILLING

12 medium-sized peaches

3 tablespoons honey or sugar

1 teaspoon cinnamon

¼ cup salted margarine, cut into small pieces

1 tablespoon lemon juice

BATTER

2 cups flour

1½ teaspoons baking powder

pinch salt

2 tablespoons sugar

¼ cup salted margarine

1 cup water

Preparing the filling: Wash and peel peaches. Cut peaches in half and remove the pit. Cut fruit into slices, and arrange them in a lightly greased 7x11-inch loaf pan. Pour honey over the fruit, sprinkle cinnamon and margarine over the peaches and honey, and drizzle the lemon juice over all.

Preparing the batter: Sift flour and baking powder into a bowl. Add salt, sugar, margarine, and water. Mix all ingredients into a sticky, dough-like batter. By spoonfuls, spread batter over peaches.

Bake in a preheated 350°F (180°C) oven for about 40 minutes, until the fruit is soft and the top is lightly browned. Serve warm.

Variation: Instead of peaches, use other fruits, such as apricots, apples, or plums.

Note: If you plan to rewarm the cake, bake it in a smaller pan (you can use a disposable one) so the cake will be higher. Refrigerate until rewarming.

CAKES WITH FRUIT

One-Bowl Peach Cake

A light summer fruit cake, the base is a beaten batter, decorated with a layer of peach slices. This cake can also be baked with two layers of dough and a layer of fruit between them as well as on top. For variation, you may use apricots, apples, or other fruit. This cake freezes well.

1½ cups sugar
1½ cups salted margarine
6 eggs
3 tablespoons lemon juice
rind of one lemon, grated finely
pinch salt
3 cups flour
1 teaspoon baking powder
about 1½ pounds peaches

♀ In a bowl, combine all ingredients *except* the fruit, mixing well.

♀ Lightly grease a 9x13-inch pan. Pour in cake batter; level the top with a spatula.

♀ Wash and dry the fruit. Slice and arrange on top of batter in even rows.

♀ Bake in a preheated 350°F (180°C) oven for 50 minutes until golden brown.

Dairy Peach Cake

This fruit cake makes an outstanding dessert, crowned with whipped cream and a colorful layer of jellied fruit. This cake does not freeze well.

CAKE

2 cups flour
1 teaspoon baking powder
¾ cup sugar
½ cup oil
2 eggs
¼ cup water
½ lemon — juice and grated rind
pinch salt

TOPPING

1 cup sweet whipping cream
1 tablespoon sugar
1 pound peaches — ripe, fresh (peeled, pitted, and halved) or
    canned, drained

FINISHING TOUCH

1 package peach or apricot jello

Preparing the cake: Sift flour and baking powder into a bowl. Add remaining ingredients, and mix into a smooth batter. Lightly grease a 7x11-inch baking pan or a 10-inch round pan. Pour batter into the pan, smoothing top with a spatula.

Bake in a preheated 350°F (180°C) oven for about 20 minutes. (Insert a toothpick to check if ready. If it comes out clean, the cake is ready.) Remove baked cake from oven, and cool to room temperature.

Preparing the topping: Whip the cream, gradually adding the sugar until it holds its shape. Spread the whipped cream over the cooled cake. Arrange fruit slices over whipped cream.

Preparing the finishing touch: Prepare the jellied desert according to the directions on the package. When cool but only partially jelled, pour over the fruit.

Refrigerate until ready to serve.

CAKES WITH FRUIT

Banana Cake

This tasty cake, full of bananas, came to Israel from America. It is easy to make and has a wonderful aroma and texture. This cake freezes well.

1 cup unsalted margarine (or butter)
1½ cups sugar
pinch salt
3 eggs
about ½ cup orange juice (or milk)
4 large, ripe bananas, mashed
grated rind of 1 lemon
4 cups flour
3 teaspoons baking powder

In a bowl, beat margarine with sugar. Beat in other ingredients.

Lightly grease a 10-inch round baking pan or two 9x5-inch loaf pans. Pour batter into baking pan.

Bake for 60–70 minutes at 350°F (180°C). As the cake bakes, it will crack along the top. When cake is nicely browned, insert a toothpick to check if done. It is ready when the toothpick comes out clean.

Dairy Fruit Strips

A wonderfully light cake, particularly fitting for hot summer days. The term "strips" fits this cake better, since it consists of a very thin flaky base covered with rows of sliced seasonal fruit smothered in a tasty dairy topping. You can use apricots, apples, plums, and so on. This low cake is an instant favorite. Freezes well.

DOUGH

2 cups flour

8 ounces cream cheese (5% fat)

1 cup salted margarine, cubed

FILLING

2 pounds fresh fruit (apricots, apples, plums)

2 eggs

7 tablespoons sugar

½ teaspoon cinnamon

pinch ground cloves — optional

pinch ginger — optional

2 heaping tablespoons flour

about ⅓ cup milk

Preparing the dough: Sift flour into a bowl. Add cheese and margarine. Knead into a soft, pliable dough.

☙ Lightly grease a 15x10-inch baking pan. Line the pan with the dough, pressing it in evenly.

Preparing the filling: Wash and dry the fruit. You do not have to peel it. Slice and arrange the fruit on the dough in densely packed parallel rows.

☙ Put eggs, sugar, spices, flour, and milk into a bowl. Stir into a uniform mixture thick as whipped cream — you may have to adjust the amount of milk. Pour the mixture over the fruit layer.

☙ Bake in a preheated 350°F (180°C) oven about 50 minutes until lightly browned.

☙ Cake is best served fresh from the oven.

Lemon Meringue Pie, p. 191; English Cake, p. 176

Cherry Cheese Cake

Cheese lovers do not let any opportunity for enriching a cake with cheese escape them. This time we have a cheesecake with a flaky pastry base and a cherry cheese filling. This cake freezes well.

about 2 tablespoons bread crumbs

DOUGH

2 heaping cups flour
1 teaspoon baking powder
½ cup butter or margarine, cubed
⅓ cup sugar
1 egg

FILLING

½ cup almonds, finely ground
1 teaspoon cinnamon
pinch cloves
pinch nutmeg
1 pound cream cheese (9% fat)
1 lemon — juice and finely grated rind
4 eggs
¾ cup sugar
1 package instant vanilla-flavored pudding mix
1 cup sweet whipping cream
1 pound canned sweet pitted cherries

Preparing the dough: Sift flour and baking powder into a bowl. Add cubed margarine (or butter), sugar, and egg. Knead into a soft dough. (If too dry, add a tablespoon or two of liquid.) Gather into a ball. Refrigerate for about 30 minutes.

☞ Lightly grease a 10-inch round baking pan. Spread bread crumbs on the bottom.

☞ Roll the dough into a circle about 12½ inches in diameter. Line the sides and bottom of the pan with the dough, leaving an edge slightly higher than the pan.

☞ Bake in a preheated 350°F (180°C) oven for 15 minutes until golden. Dough will be partially baked.

Preparing the filling: Put ground almonds in a bowl. Add cinnamon, cloves, and nutmeg, and mix with almonds.

🍳 Put the cheese in a different bowl, and mix in the lemon, eggs, sugar, pudding mix, and whipping cream. Taste the mixture, and adjust flavorings, if necessary.

🍳 Over the partially baked crust, sprinkle the almond mixture. Pour half of the cheese mixture over it. Put two-thirds of the cherries over the cheese. Cover all with the other half of the cheese mixture. Distribute the remaining cherries on the top, pressing lightly to hold in place.

🍳 Return pan to oven, and bake 50 minutes more. Turn off the oven. Let cake stand in the oven, with the door open, for about 20 minutes to cool.

Carrot Cake I

A cake with a taste reminiscent of honey cake. Its secret is in the ingredients — nuts and carrots! This cake freezes well.

⅓ cup salted margarine, at room temperature
1¼ cup sugar
2 large eggs
1 teaspoon baking soda
2 cups flour
pinch salt
½ teaspoon ground cloves
1 teaspoon cinnamon
½ cup raisins
½ cup ground walnuts
1 cup carrots, finely grated

🍳 Beat margarine until light. Add sugar and eggs. Beat in remaining ingredients, mixing well.

🍳 Lightly flour a 9x5-inch baking pan, and pour in the batter.

🍳 Bake in a preheated 350°F (180°C) oven for 40 minutes.

Cherry Pudding Cake

Similar to regular cherry pie but even richer. The flaky pie crust is covered by a layer of cherries, fresh or canned, mixed with a tasty fruit whip and topped with a meringue layer. This cake does not freeze well.

DOUGH

1 cup salted margarine

½ cup sugar

5 egg yolks

½ cup ground almonds

1½ cups flour

1 teaspoon baking powder

1 teaspoon lemon rind

PUDDING FILLING

½ cup dry red wine mixed with

½ cup water

2 tablespoons sugar

2 heaping tablespoons cornstarch

1 cup juice from preserved cherries

pinch cinnamon

16 oz. canned sweet pitted cherries

TOPPING

5 egg whites

½ cup sugar

Preparing the dough: Cube margarine, and beat into the sugar. Stir in egg yolks and almonds. Knead the dough, and thoroughly work in flour, baking powder, and lemon rind.

☙ Line a 10-inch round pan with the dough, leaving some dough extending a bit beyond the edge of the pan.

☙ Bake in preheated 350°F (180°C) oven for about 15 minutes; crust will be partially done. Remove from oven.

Preparing the filling: Pour the wine and water into a saucepan. Bring to boil. In a separate bowl, mix cornstarch, cherry juice, and cinnamon. Pour the cornstarch mixture into the boiling wine while stirring; continue to stir until the mixture thickens. Turn off the heat.

♔ Pour the hot pudding into a bowl with the cherries, and stir lightly. Spread the fruit combination over the partially baked crust.

♔ Return pan to oven, and continue to bake at 350°F (180°C) for another 25 minutes.

Preparing the topping: Beat egg whites until firm, gradually adding sugar. Spread beaten egg whites over the cake.

♔ Lower heat to 325°F (170°C), and bake another 15 minutes until lightly browned.

Variation: Use the crust for basic Cherry Pie recipe (page 188). Put a layer of fruit and pudding over it. Cover with lattice top.

Carrot Cake II

This carrot cake is made differently from most carrot cakes: the egg whites are beaten, and the resulting cake is light and airy. The taste of this delicious cake resembles that of honey cake. This cake freezes well.

½ cup salted margarine, at room temperature
1¼ cups sugar
4 eggs, separated
1 level teaspoon cinnamon
½ teaspoon ground cloves
1½ cups carrots, finely grated
3 cups self-rising flour

♔ In a bowl, mix well margarine, ¼ cup sugar, and egg yolks. Stir in cinnamon, cloves, and grated carrots.

♔ In a separate bowl, beat egg whites until peaks are firm while gradually adding the remaining cup of sugar. Gently fold the beaten egg whites into the carrot mixture. Using broad strokes, fold in the flour.

♔ Pour cake batter into a greased, 10-inch round pan.

♔ Bake in a preheated 350°F (180°C) oven for about 50 minutes until nicely browned.

Cherry Pie

Cherry pie has a place of pride among the fruit pies. This pie has a flaky bottom crust and a layer of jam covered with cherries. A lattice top sprinkled with powdered sugar covers all. It freezes well.

DOUGH

2¾ cups flour
3 teaspoons baking powder
1 cup salted margarine, cubed
½ cup sugar
1 egg
1 teaspoon grated lemon rind
juice of 1 orange

FILLING

2 heaping tablespoons jam (preferably cherry)
1 pound fresh sour cherries, washed and pitted
½ cup sugar

Preparing the dough: Sift flour and baking powder into a bowl. Cut margarine into flour until the texture of coarse crumbs. Mix while adding sugar, egg, lemon rind, and juice (or water) until dough is soft and pliable. Refrigerate a third of the dough.

♟ Lightly grease a 10-inch pie pan, preferably fluted. Line the pie pan with the unrefrigerated two thirds of the dough, extending it a bit higher than the edge of the pan.

♟ Bake in a preheated 350°F (180°C) oven for 15 minutes.

Assembling the pie: Spread the jam over the half-baked crust. Spread the cherries over the jam, and sprinkle the sugar over all.

♟ Roll out the third of the dough that was refrigerated into a circle a bit larger than the pie pan. Cut dough into strips ½-inch wide. Lay them in lattice pattern over the cherry layer. (You can brush crust with beaten egg.)

♟ Return the pan to the oven, and bake another 25 minutes until nicely browned.

♟ Cool and sprinkle with powdered sugar.

Streusel Cherry Cake

Make good use of the sweet-sour taste of cherries for scrumptious baking. This cake has a yeast dough base, a cherry filling, and a streussel topping. Instead of cherries, you can use apricots or plums. This cake freezes well.

DOUGH

4 cups flour
1 package dry yeast
½ + ¾ cups lukewarm milk or water
1 teaspoon vanilla
pinch salt
½ cup soft butter or margarine
1 egg
about ⅓ cup sugar

FILLING

1 cup ground almonds
about ⅓ cup sugar
2 pounds sweet cherries, washed and pitted

TOPPING

1¼ cups flour
pinch baking powder
½ cup butter or margarine
½ cup sugar

Preparing the dough: Sift flour into a bowl. Dissolve yeast in the ½ cup of milk. Pour into the flour and add all the other ingredients. Knead into a soft, smooth dough. Lightly flour the ball of dough and cover with a towel. Rise until doubled.

Lightly grease the largest baking pan you have. On a lightly floured surface, roll the dough into a rectangle about an inch longer on each side than the baking ban. Lift the dough with the help of a rolling pin, and place it in the baking pan. Press dough to all sides of pan. Let it rise for another 20 minutes.

Preparing the filling: Mix together the almonds and sugar. Sprinkle them over the dough. Cover the dough with pitted cherries.

Preparing the topping: Sift the flour and baking powder into a bowl. In a small saucepan, melt the butter and brown it slightly. Add sugar and melted butter to the flour. Work manually into a crumbly dough. Sprinkle the crumbs over the cherries. Bake in a preheated 400°F (200°C) oven for 40 minutes. Serve warm.

CAKES WITH FRUIT

Lemon Cake

An easy-to-make, delicious cake. You combine the cake's ingredients in your processor bowl (or by hand). The added touch comes with candied fruit, raisins, or almonds. The white glaze gives it a delicate lemony taste, and baked in a fluted Kugelhopf pan, it is especially appealing. This cake freezes well.

CAKE

1¼ cups margarine or butter

1½ cups sugar

4 eggs

4 cups flour

3 teaspoons baking powder

⅔ cup water or milk

grated rind of 1 lemon

½ cup candied orange peel or raisins

1 tablespoon cognac

GLAZE

4 tablespoons lemon juice

2 tablespoons water

¼ cup sugar

1 tablespoon cognac

1 cup powdered sugar

2 tablespoons chopped walnuts

Preparing the cake: Beat margarine lightly. Add eggs and sugar. Continue to beat until thoroughly mixed. Sift flour and baking powder, and add to mixture. Pour in liquids; add lemon rind and orange peel or raisins. Mix until batter is smooth.

Lightly grease a Kugelhopf pan, a 9x5-inch baking pan, or a tube pan. Spoon batter into pan.

Bake in a preheated 375°F (190°C) oven for about 75 minutes. Insert a toothpick to check if cake is done; if it comes out clean, cake is ready.

Preparing the glaze: In a small saucepan, put 2 tablespoons lemon juice, water, and sugar. Bring to boil. Remove from heat, and add cognac. (For variation, use orange juice in place of cognac.)

Decorating the cake: Drizzle the glaze over the cake. Mix the remaining 2 tablespoons of lemon juice with powdered sugar, and drizzle over the cake. Immediately sprinkle the nuts on top.

Lemon Meringue Pie [picture on page 182]

A delectable, light pie, with a lemon-flavored pudding filling. The base is a pie crust, the top a meringue. This pie does not freeze well.

DOUGH

2¾ cups flour

1 cup salted margarine, cubed

½ cup sugar

about ¼ cup orange juice or water

FILLING

6 tablespoons cornstarch

1 cup sugar

1 lemon — juice and finely grated rind

2 cups water

7 egg yolks

1 tablespoon unsalted margarine

TOPPING

7 egg whites

1 cup sugar

Preparing the dough: The crust ingredients are enough for two bottom crusts for 9-inch pie plates or one crust for a 9x13-inch baking pan.

♕ Sift flour into a bowl. Add margarine. Add sugar and juice. Work everything into a dough. Cover the ball of dough, and refrigerate for 30 minutes.

♕ Lightly grease a baking pan or pie tin. Line it with the dough, pressing it evenly.

♕ Bake in a 350°F (180°C) oven for about 20 minutes until golden. Cool.

Preparing the filling: In a saucepan, mix cornstarch, sugar, and lemon. Stir in water. Cook over medium heat, stirring constantly with a wooden spoon, until the mixture thickens into a pudding. Turn off heat. Remove pan from stove. Stir in egg yolks. Fold in softened margarine. Spread the filling over the baked crust.

Preparing the topping: In a separate bowl, beat egg whites until firm, gradually adding the sugar. Gently spread beaten egg whites over the filling. Return pan to the oven, and bake for an additional 15 minutes until top is delicately browned.

♕ Refrigerate until served.

CAKES WITH FRUIT

Flaky Apricot Pie

A summer cake, delicious and easy to prepare. This pie has a flaky base, an apricot layer, and a jam glaze that gives it a sheen. You can use peaches, instead, with similar results. This pie freezes well.

DOUGH

2 cups flour
1½ teaspoons baking powder
⅓ cup sugar
¼ cup salted margarine
1 egg
about ⅓ cup juice or water
½ teaspoon lemon rind or vanilla extract

FILLING

2 pounds apricots
3 tablespoons sugar
3 tablespoons apricot jam
1 tablespoon hot water

Preparing the dough: Sift flour with baking powder. Add sugar and margarine. Begin to work dough into crumbs. Add the eggs and juice (or water) alternatingly, and knead into a soft, pliable dough. The amount of liquid may have to be adjusted as you work. Flavor with lemon rind or vanilla.

♗ Lightly grease a 12x7½-inch baking pan with the dough.

♗ Bake for 10 minutes.

Preparing the filling: Scald the fruit in boiling water. Peel and divide each apricot into four pieces. Arrange fruit on dough, with the rounded side up. Sprinkle with sugar.

♗ Bake at 375°F (190°C) for 30 minutes.

♗ Mix the jam with the water, and drizzle it over the almost-baked fruit. Return pan to oven, and bake 10 minutes more until nicely browned.

♗ Cut into squares and serve fresh.

Variation: Instead of fresh apricots, you can use canned. Make the dough as described, and line the baking pan with it. Arrange apricot halves over it. Add a layer of streusel crumbs to the top, made as follows:

CRUMBS

½ cup sugar

¼ cup flour

½ teaspoon cinnamon

¼ cup chopped walnuts

¼ cup salted margarine

Combine all ingredients in a bowl. Mix well. Sprinkle crumbs over apricots.

Bake in a 375°F (190°C) for about 30 minutes, until the crumbs are lightly brown and crispy.

CAKES WITH FRUIT

Apricot Cheese Cake

A very pretty, easy-to-make cake. The cake consists of a flaky, almond-tasting bottom layer, a high cheese filling, and a crown of apricots and crumbs browned in the baking. This cake freezes well.

DOUGH

1½ cups flour

1 teaspoon baking powder

⅓ cup margarine or butter

rind of a lemon, finely grated

½ cup sugar

½ cup grated almonds — optional

1 egg

FILLING

1 cup margarine or butter

1 cup sugar

4 eggs, separated

1½ pounds cream cheese (5% fat)

juice of 1 medium-sized lemon

1 package vanilla pudding mix

1 teaspoon rum flavoring

1 medium-size can apricots

Preparing the dough: Sift flour and baking powder into a bowl. Add remaining ingredients, and knead into a well-combined dough. Refrigerate dough for an hour.

Remove dough from refrigerator, and separate a third for the topping. Put that part in the freezer until needed.

Lightly grease a 10-inch round pan. Line it with the other two-thirds of the dough, pressing it evenly.

Bake in a preheated 350°F (180°C) oven for about 10 minutes. The crust will be partially baked.

Preparing the filling: Place margarine in a bowl, and beat until creamy. Add ½ cup sugar and egg yolks while beating. Add the cream cheese and mix well. Continue to beat, and add juice, pudding, and rum.

In a separate bowl, beat the egg whites until peaks are firm, gradually adding remaining sugar. Fold beaten egg whites into the cheese mixture. Pour cheese mixture over the partially baked dough.

Drain canned apricots well. Arrange apricots around the top of the cake, one circle near the edge, an inner circle at the center.

Take the reserved dough out of the freezer, and grate it into coarse crumbs over the apricots.

Return the cake to the oven, and bake for about 80 minutes. Insert a toothpick to test if cake is done. When toothpick comes out clean, cake is ready. When cake is fully baked, turn off the heat, and leave the cake in the oven about 20 minutes more to cool.

Variation: You can add 1½ tablespoons cocoa to the dough for a brown base.

Note: With such a large amount of cheese filling, it is worthwhile putting waxed paper around the baked dough to support the filling during baking. The filling will rise during the baking and sink a bit as the cake cools.

CAKES WITH FRUIT

Coconut Dominoes

A great cake arranged in layers — dark–white–dark — two brown cake layers with coconut between them. A chocolate-halvah frosting tops it off. Freezes well.

CAKE

6 eggs, separated

1¼ cups sugar

1 tablespoon oil

3 tablespoons cognac or rum

2½ tablespoons cocoa

4 heaping tablespoons self-rising flour

1½ cups flaked coconut

FROSTING

4 tablespoons sugar

3 tablespoons cocoa

2 tablespoons water

4 ounces halvah

Preparing the cake: Put egg whites into a bowl. Gradually adding 1 cup sugar, beat until peaks are firm.

♗ In a separate bowl, beat egg yolks with the remaining sugar until light. Stir in oil, cognac, cocoa, and flour, and mix thoroughly. Gently fold in 2 tablespoons of beaten egg white.

♗ Fold the coconut into the beaten egg whites.

♗ Line a 9x11-inch baking pan or a 10-inch round pan with baking parchment. Pour in half of the dark batter. Over it, pour the coconut mixture, spreading it with a spatula. Cover that with the remaining dark cake batter — pouring the batter tablespoon by tablespoon. Carefully, spread it evenly.

♗ Bake in a preheated 350°F (180°C) oven for about 45 minutes. Insert a toothpick to check if cake is done. When toothpick comes out clean, the cake is ready.

Preparing the frosting: In a saucepan, mix sugar, cocoa, and water. Add the halvah, cut into cubes. Over medium heat, melt all into a smooth syrup. Pour the hot syrup over the baked cake, spreading it evenly with a spatula.

Layered Coconut Cake

An attractive, tasty cake. The delicate, brown base is covered with a high coconut layer topped with chocolate. This cake freezes well.

BASE

8 egg yolks

8 tablespoons sugar

¼ cup oil

1 tablespoon instant coffee powder

3 tablespoons boiling water

8 tablespoons self-rising flour

FILLING

8 egg whites

1 cup sugar

1 teaspoon vanilla

7 ounces flaked coconut

2 tablespoons self-rising flour

TOPPING

3 tablespoons sugar

3 tablespoons cocoa

3½ ounces semi-sweet baking chocolate, broken into pieces

3 tablespoons wine or water

⅓ cup unsalted margarine, cubed

Preparing the base: In a bowl, stir together egg yolks, sugar, and oil. Dissolve the coffee in the boiling water, and pour into yolk mixture. Add flour, and mix well.

♀ Line a 9x13-inch baking pan with baking parchment, or grease pan lightly. Spread the batter in the pan.

Preparing the filling: Beat the egg whites until firm, gradually adding the sugar. Fold in vanilla, coconut, and flour. Pour over the base layer.

♀ Bake in a 350°F (180°C) oven about 45 minutes until coconut filling is lightly browned. Remove pan from the oven.

Preparing the topping: Put sugar, cocoa, chocolate pieces, and wine or water into a saucepan. Stir over a low flame until ingredients melt and thicken. Remove from heat, and add margarine. Stir until it becomes a uniform syrup. Pour it over the cake. Refrigerate.

Wonderful Coconut Bars

A two-layer cake with a delicate base and a wonderful coconut filling. You slice this cake into long bars for serving. This cake freezes well.

BATTER

10 egg yolks

10 tablespoons sugar

½ cup oil

2½ tablespoons vinegar

2 teaspoons vanilla

12 tablespoons self-rising flour

FILLING

10 egg whites

1 cup sugar

2 teaspoons vanilla

4 ounces chocolate, grated

4 ounces flaked coconut

Preparing the batter: Place all batter ingredients into a bowl, and mix well.

☞ Line a 9x13-inch baking pan with baking parchment. Spread batter in pan evenly with a spatula.

☞ Bake in a 350°F (180°C) oven for about 10 minutes until golden.

Preparing the filling: Beat egg whites until firm, gradually adding sugar. Fold in vanilla, grated chocolate, and flaked coconut. Spread coconut mixture over the half-baked layer.

☞ Bake at 300°F (160°C) for about 45 minutes.

Coconut Crown Cake

A scrumptious two-layer cake. The light, flaky base is covered with a layer of jam and crowned with a sweet coconut layer. This cake freezes well.

DOUGH

1½ cups salted margarine

1 cup sugar

1 teaspoon vanilla extract

6 egg yolks

1 cup water or orange juice

4 cups flour

3 teaspoons baking powder

GLAZE

1 cup jam

1 tablespoon cocoa dissolved in 3 tablespoons boiling water

TOPPING

6 egg whites

1 cup sugar

1 cup coconut

Preparing the dough: Beat margarine and sugar well. Mix in vanilla extract, egg yolks, and liquid. Knead the dough while adding flour and baking powder.

Lightly grease a 15 x 10-inch baking pan and, with moistened hands, line it with the dough.

Bake in a preheated 350°F (180°C) oven for about 15 minutes. Crust will not be fully baked.

Preparing the glaze: Put the jam into a bowl. Pour the cocoa mixture over it, and mix well. Pour over the partially baked dough.

Preparing the topping: Beat egg whites until firm, gradually adding sugar. Gently fold in coconut. Spread this mixture over the jam.

Bake at 325°F (170°C) for another 45 minutes until nicely golden.

CAKES WITH FRUIT

Coconut Cake Rolls

Narrow, long cake rolls, with a delicate golden tint, filled with wonderful sweetened coconut. A fine layer of powdered sugar dusts the top. Freezes well.

DOUGH

3½ cups flour
½ packet dry yeast
½ cup lukewarm water
1¼ cups salted margarine
2 egg yolks
2 tablespoons sugar
pinch salt

FILLING

3 cups flaked coconut
2 egg whites
1½ cups sugar
1 lemon — juice and finely grated rind

TOPPING

powdered sugar

Preparing the dough: Sift flour into a bowl. Dissolve yeast in lukewarm water, and pour into a well in the flour. Add remaining ingredients. Knead into a pliable, easy-to-roll dough. Divide into six parts.

Line two 9x13-inch baking pans with baking parchment. Roll each piece of dough into a rectangle 8x13 inches.

Preparing the filling: Put coconut into a bowl. In a separate bowl, beat egg whites until firm, gradually adding sugar. Fold coconut into beaten whites. Gently add lemon juice and rind.

Divide filling into six portions. Put one-sixth of the filling on the center of each dough rectangle. Fold into a roll by bringing the right-hand long side over the filling, then folding the left side over it. You will have a long, narrow roll. Place in baking pan, seam-side down, three rolls to a pan.

Bake in a preheated 350°F (180°C) oven for 35 minutes or until lightly browned.

Remove from oven, and use a fine-meshed sifter to sift powdered sugar over the top. Cut into thin slices, and serve fresh.

No-Bake Coconut Cake Roll

A delightful, easy-to-make cake roll. The cake is made from crushed cookies flavored with cocoa and a coconut filling. This sweet cake roll should be stored in the freezer.

CAKE ROLL

8 ounces plain cookies, finely crushed

½ cup water

½ cup sugar

2 tablespoons cocoa

2 tablespoons wine or juice

¼ cup unsalted margarine

FILLING

½ cup salted margarine, cubed

½ cup sugar

1 cup flaked coconut

2 tablespoons water

Preparing the cake roll: Put crushed cookies into a bowl. Pour water into a saucepan. Stir in sugar, cocoa, wine, and margarine. Cook, stirring constantly, over medium heat until all ingredients have dissolved and you have a smooth syrup. Pour over crushed cookies, and combine thoroughly.

♙ Draw a 8x14 inch rectangle in the middle of a piece of baking parchment. Spread the crushed cookie mixture evenly within the rectangle.

Preparing the filling: Put margarine, sugar, coconut, and water into a saucepan. Stirring constantly, cook over medium heat until margarine dissolves. Spoon coconut filling over the crushed cookie layer.

♙ Lift the edge of one of the long sides of the baking parchment, and roll the cake over to the other side in jelly-roll fashion. Wrap the roll in freezer paper. It is best to cut it in two for easier storage. Freeze until served.

♙ Remove from freezer a few minutes before serving to slightly thaw for easier slicing. Cut thin slices, and serve cold.

CAKES WITH FRUIT

Classic Apple Layer Cake

A wonderful apple cake with two yeast-dough layers — and in the middle, a moist apple filling. You can use a lattice top if you wish. In addition, this dough is good for filled crescents, rogelach, and other items. This cake freezes well.

DOUGH

3½ cups flour

1 cup salted margarine, cubed

⅓ cup sugar

pinch salt

3 egg yolks

1 cake compressed yeast

about ½ cup orange juice or water

FILLING

3 pounds baking apples

½ cup sugar

1 teaspoon cinnamon

¼ cup bread crumbs

TOPPING

1 egg, beaten

powdered sugar

Preparing the dough: Sift flour into a bowl. Cut margarine into flour until pieces are size of small peas. Add sugar, salt, egg yolks, and yeast dissolved in juice or water. Knead all into a pliable, easy-to-roll dough. The amount of liquid may have to be adjusted as you work. Cover the dough, and refrigerate for one hour.

♗ Lightly flour a work surface. Divide the dough into two parts. Lightly grease a 9x13-inch baking pan. Roll one portion of dough into a rectangle the size of the pan; press dough into pan.

Preparing the filling: Wash, dry, and core the apples. Grate apples coarsely. Add sugar and cinnamon. Squeeze lightly, and pour off excess liquid. Sprinkle bread crumbs over dough in pan. Arrange the apples over the crumbs in a uniform layer. Roll the remaining portion of dough into a rectangle slightly larger than the baking pan. Place it over the apples.

♗ Brush the top with beaten egg. Prick well with a fork, so steam can escape during baking.

Bake in a preheated 350°F (180°C) oven for about 45 minutes until nicely browned. Sprinkle powdered sugar over baked cake, using a fine-meshed sifter.

Variations:

1) Cover apple filling with lattice top. Roll second portion of dough into a rectangle slightly larger than the baking pan. Cut ½-inch wide diagonal strips of dough. Place strips on the cake in a diagonal lattice pattern. Brush the strips with beaten egg, and bake 45 minutes at 350°F (180°C).

2) Instead of fresh apples, use steamed apples. Put the grated apple, sugar, and cinnamon into a saucepan. Cook uncovered over low to medium heat, until the liquids evaporate (about 20 minutes). Spoon the steamed apples over the dough covered with bread crumbs. Continue to bake as above.

CAKES WITH FRUIT

Rich Apple Pie

A wonderful apple pie whose richly spiced filling rests on a base of ground hazelnuts and flaky pastry. This pie freezes well.

DOUGH

2½ cups flour
1 cup salted margarine, cubed
2 eggs
1 teaspoon vanilla
pinch salt
½ cup sugar
⅔ cup ground hazelnuts

FILLING

3 pounds baking apples
1 lemon — juice and finely grated rind
1 teaspoon cinnamon
½ teaspoon nutmeg
½ teaspoon ginger
½ teaspoon ground cloves
¾ cup raisins
½ cup sugar

TOPPING

3–4 tablespoons soft jam

Preparing the dough: Sift flour into bowl. Cut in margarine until pieces are size of small peas. Add eggs, vanilla, salt, and sugar. Knead into a dough, shape into a ball, and cover with plastic wrap. Refrigerate 30 minutes.

Separate one-third of the dough, and set it aside. Lightly grease a 10-inch round pan. Line it with the remaining two-thirds of the dough, with edges extending about 1 inch beyond side of pan.

Sprinkle the ground nuts over the dough. Bake the crust for about 15 minutes at 350°F (180°C).

Preparing the filling: Peel, core, and quarter the apples. Cut quarters into slices, and sprinkle with lemon juice. Add lemon rind and spices to the apples. Scald raisins in boiling water, drain well, and add to apples. Stir in sugar, and mix all thoroughly. Put filling over the ground nuts in the partially baked crust.

♗ On a floured surface, roll the reserved one-third of the dough into a circle slightly larger than the diameter of the baking pan. Lift with help of rolling pin, and place dough over filling. Pinch edges of the two crusts together. Prick dough well to allow steam to escape during baking.

♗ Bake in a preheated 400°F (200°C) oven for 40 minutes. Turn off oven.

♗ Brush top of baked pie with jam, and return to turned-off oven. Let stand for 15 minutes.

Dairy or Pareve Apple Upside-Down Cake

A scrumptious, attractive, interesting cake. As an upside-down cake, you first put the grated apple filling in the pan and then spread the batter on top. After baking, you turn the cake out with the apples on top. Whipped cream or nondairy whipped topping covers the baked cake. This cake freezes well.

FILLING

2½ pounds baking apples

1 cup sugar

1 heaping tablespoon cinnamon

4 tablespoons cookie or bread crumbs

CAKE

5 eggs, separated

5 tablespoons sugar

2 tablespoons oil

½ lemon — juice and finely grated rind

5 tablespoons self-rising flour

TOPPING

1 cup whipping cream or nondairy whipped topping

2 tablespoons sugar

DECORATION

3 baking apples

3 tablespoons sugar

½ cup water

1 tablespoon lemon juice

candied cherries — optional

walnut halves — optional

Preparing the filling: Wash, dry, and core apples. Grate coarsely. Add sugar and cinnamon. Mix well.

Line a 9x13-inch pan with baking parchment. Spread the apple filling evenly over it. Sprinkle crumbs over apples.

Preparing the cake: Beat egg yolks well with 1 tablespoon sugar. Beat in oil and lemon. In a separate bowl, beat egg whites until firm, gradually adding remaining sugar. Gently fold into egg yolk mixture. Using broad strokes, fold in flour. Pour batter over apples, smoothing top with spatula.

☕ Bake in a preheated 350°F (180°C) oven for about 45 minutes until nicely browned.

☕ Cool cake, and carefully turn out over a tray. Peel off baking parchment.

Preparing the topping: Beat whipping cream or nondairy topping while gradually adding sugar. Cover baked apples evenly.

Decorating cake: Peel apples, and cut into ¼-inch slices. Put into a saucepan, and add sugar, water, and lemon juice. Cook over medium heat for 5 minutes to partially soften.

☕ Place apple slices over whipped cream. In the middle of each slice you can put a candied cherry or walnut half. Refrigerate until served.

CAKES WITH FRUIT

Layered Apple Cake

Wonderfully light, this cake has a sponge-cake base with an apple filling mixed with a jelled dessert. Whipped topping covers all. You can add chocolate sprinkles, candied cherries, or nuts. This cake does not freeze well.

SPONGE CAKE BASE

4 eggs, separated

4 tablespoons sugar

½ lemon — juice and finely grated rind

1 tablespoon oil

4 tablespoons self-rising flour

APPLE FILLING

1½ pounds baking apples

½ cup sugar

¾ cup water

juice of ½ lemon

1 package lemon-flavor jelled dessert

TOPPING

1 cup whipping cream or nondairy whipped topping

2 tablespoons sugar

Preparing the base: In a bowl, beat egg yolks, 2 tablespoons sugar, lemon juice, rind, and oil. In a separate bowl, beat egg whites until firm, gradually adding the remaining sugar. Fold beaten whites gently into yolk mixture. With broad strokes, fold in flour.

☺ Lightly grease an 11-inch round pan. Pour batter into pan.

☺ Bake in a preheated 350°F (180°C) oven for about 35 minutes until lightly browned. Insert a toothpick to check if done. It is ready when the toothpick comes out clean. Cool on a rack.

Preparing the filling: Peel, core, and quarter apples. Put into pot, and add sugar, water, and lemon. Begin to cook. After water boils, cook over medium heat for about 15 minutes — until apples are soft. Puree the cooked apples.

☺ In a separate bowl, prepare the lemon jelled dessert according to the package instructions, but use only 1 cup water. When the mixture begins to become firm, mix in the apple puree. Pour over baked cake, and refrigerate 2 hours.

Preparing the topping: Beat whipped cream while gradually adding sugar, until it holds its shape. Spread over top and sides of cake. Decorate. Refrigerate.

Flaky Pastry Plum Cake

This delicious, tart pastry has a crispy base and flakes of dough on top. Easy to make, it is best served fresh. A small cake, it is finished in a wink. This cake freezes well.

DOUGH

3 cups flour

2 teaspoons baking powder

1 cup salted margarine, cubed

1 egg

½ cup sugar

about 2 tablespoons water or juice

FILLING

3–4 tablespoons jam — optional

1½ pounds plums

½ cup sugar

1 teaspoon cinnamon — optional

Preparing the dough: Sift flour and baking powder into a bowl. Add margarine. Begin to knead into a dough while adding the other ingredients. Knead until dough is soft and easy to roll. Divide dough into three equal parts. Place one third in the freezer. Refrigerate the other two thirds for an hour.

꒳ Lightly flour a 12x7-inch baking pan. Press the refrigerated dough evenly into the pan.

Assembling the cake: Wash, dry, and pit the plums. Cut them in half.

꒳ Spread jam evenly over the dough. Place the plums, cut side up, on the jam in closely packed rows. Sprinkle sugar mixed with cinnamon over the plums. If you did not spread jam on the dough, add another ½ cup sugar. Take the reserved third of the dough out of the freezer, and grate it over the plums, covering them evenly.

꒳ Bake in a preheated 350°F (180°C) oven for about 40 minutes until lightly browned.

Plum Torte

A light, tasty plum cake. The cake base, light and airy, is covered by a layer of plums and topped with a dusting of powdered sugar. You can also serve with mounds of whipped cream. This cake freezes well.

4 eggs, separated
1 cup salted margarine
1 cup sugar
1 lemon — juice and grated rind
1¾ cups self-rising flour
2 pounds fresh plums, washed, dried, and pitted
powdered sugar

♔ Combine egg yolks, margarine, and ½ cup sugar in a bowl. Beat well. Mix in the lemon juice, rind, and flour.

♔ In a separate bowl, beat egg whites until stiff while gradually adding remaining sugar. Fold beaten egg whites into yolk mixture.

♔ Lightly grease a 9x13-inch pan, and pour in batter. Spread evenly.

♔ Cut plums in half, and arrange close together over cake batter. Bake in a pre-heated 350°F (180°C) for 45 minutes.

♔ Sprinkle top with powdered sugar. Serve freshly baked.

Dried-Fruit Cake

A tasty, easy-to-make cake whose ingredients you mix all at once. You can add chopped fruits to make the cake even more interesting. Bake in a long pan or a small round or rectangular one. This cake is especially fitting for Tu B'Shevat. This cake freezes well.

4 eggs
1½ cups sugar
1 cup oil
1 cup juice or water
4 cups flour
4 teaspoons baking powder
1 cup dried fruit (dates, figs, papaya, raisins, etc.)
½ cup chopped almonds or walnuts
rind of 1 lemon or orange, grated fine
1 teaspoon vanilla or almond extract

♔ Put all ingredients into a bowl, and mix them together thoroughly.

♔ Lightly grease a round 10-inch pan, and pour in batter.

♔ Bake in a preheated 350°F (180°C) oven for about 45 minutes. Insert a toothpick to check if cake is done. When toothpick comes out clean, the cake is ready.

AMONG THE most beloved, basic pastries are those made from yeast dough. To prepare yeast cakes takes time, since the dough must rise. Yet from a single batch you can make many cakes. Yeast cakes are wonderful when fresh and they also freeze well. Children and adults love them. They are filling and are favorites even without thick frostings. Yeast dough can be made in a number of ways: with fresh yeast, refrigerated yeast, dry granulated yeast, and so on. You can make rolled yeast cakes with fillings such as cocoa, cinnamon, poppy seed, walnuts, cheese, and more. The dough can be formed into many shapes, such as crescents, rosettes, or buns.

Yeast Cakes

Layered Yeast Dough

Layered yeast dough, with a wonderful texture in each layer. Preparation involves a number of advance stages, since it has to be worked and folded like puff pastry. This dough freezes well.

8 cups flour
2 ounces yeast
2 to 2½ cups lukewarm water
1 egg
2 egg yolks
½ cup sugar
2 cups salted margarine, cubed
pinch salt

Layered dough can be made in two ways:

METHOD ONE: Sift the flour into a bowl. Dissolve the yeast in about ½ cup of water (from the 2½ cups), and let stand for about 10 minutes as it begins to swell. Make a well in the flour and add the yeast, egg, yolks, sugar, 1 cup of the cubed margarine, and salt. Knead the dough until smooth and elastic, adding the remainder of the water as needed. Shape the dough into a ball.

♟ Using the dough hook of an electric mixture enhances the airiness of the dough.

♟ Lightly flour a working surface. Divide the ball of dough into four parts. Roll each part into a square about 10x10 inches. Divide the remaining margarine into four parts. Spread margarine on top of each square of dough. Fold each sheet of dough as if it were an envelope. (First fold a third of the dough towards the middle, and fold the opposite third over the first fold. Give the dough a quarter turn. Then fold one-third dough toward the middle; then fold the opposite third over the first fold.)

♟ Lightly flour the dough envelopes. Cover with a kitchen towel, and let rise for about an hour at room temperature or in the refrigerator. Roll the dough envelopes a second time, and fold once again into envelopes. Let stand for 10 minutes; repeat the rolling and folding a third time. The dough is ready for use.

METHOD TWO: Cut the margarine into two cups of the flour (out of the total amount) until you can form a ball of oily dough. Wrap in waxed paper and place in refrigerator.

♟ Dissolve the yeast in ½ cup of water (from the total amount), and add 1 tablespoon of sugar (also from the full amount). Let stand for 10 minutes.

👨‍🍳 Place in a large bowl for kneading with the remainder of the flour, egg, yolks, sugar, and salt. Pour in the dissolved yeast, and begin to knead the dough, adding the remaining water as necessary. Shape the dough into a ball. Lightly flour the ball of dough, cover with a kitchen towel, and let rise for about an hour.

👨‍🍳 Lightly flour a work surface. Divide the ball of dough into four parts. Roll each part into a square 8x8 inches. Divide the oily ball of dough into four parts. Spread one part of the oily ball of dough on *half* of the surface of each of the dough squares, and fold the square into two rectangles measuring 8x4 inches. Roll the rectangle again to the size of the original square. Repeat this action three more times. Refrigerate the dough envelopes for 10 minutes. Repeat these steps of rolling and folding twice more. After the final folding, allow the layered dough to rest for 15 minutes in the refrigerator. The dough is ready for use.

Layered Yeast Dough Cakes
[picture on page 218]

Layered yeast dough can be turned into many types of cakes. You can bake loaf cakes or sweet rolls. You can make rolled cakes and fill them with cocoa, cinnamon, cheese, or even a mixture of vanilla and sugar. You can spread the dough with jam or margarine, add raisins and/or bits of nuts — each giving you a different nuance. The dough is wonderful for making crescents and, again, you can use a variety of fillings. The same dough can be used for cheese pockets, and why not? You can add a glaze with beaten egg and sprinkled sesame seeds or broken almonds. Another possibility is to drizzle warmed jam over all. Whatever fits the occasion and your taste. All these cakes freeze well.

DOUGH
Layered Yeast Dough, page 214

CHOCOLATE FILLING (FOR 2 CAKE ROLLS OR SWEET BUNS)
¼ cup cocoa
1 cup sugar
1 tablespoon grated lemon rind
1 teaspoon vanilla extract — optional

CINNAMON FILLING (FOR 2 CAKE ROLLS OR SWEET BUNS)
3 tablespoons jam
2 tablespoons cinnamon
1½ cups sugar
⅔ cup raisins

NUT FILLING (FOR 2 CAKE ROLLS OR CRESCENTS)

4 generous tablespoons honey or jam

1 pound hazelnuts (or part almonds)

½ pound candied orange peel (or raisins)

1½ cups sugar

CHEESE FILLING (FOR 2 CAKE ROLLS OR POCKETS)

1 pound cream cheese

1½ cups sugar

2 egg yolks

2 teaspoons vanilla extract

⅔ cup raisins — optional

MARZIPAN FILLING (FOR CAKE RING)

½ pound marzipan

2 egg whites

Preparing the dough: Prepare one recipe of dough according to the instructions. Separate this dough into four squares. Each square is sufficient for making one rolled cake.

Preparing cake rolls: Lightly flour a work surface. Roll each square of dough to a sheet 9x13 inches. Make the filling of your choice. Each filling recipe is enough for two cakes.

Preparing the chocolate cake rolls: In a bowl, stir cocoa, sugar, lemon rind or vanilla. You can sprinkle the filling over the dough, or spread 1½ tablespoons margarine or jam over the dough before sprinkling the filling. Roll lengthwise, jelly-roll style.

Preparing the cinnamon cake rolls: Roll out two packets of dough. Spread 1½ tablespoons of jam over the dough. In a small bowl, mix cinnamon and sugar. Sprinkle over the jam. Sprinkle the raisins. Roll lengthwise, jelly-roll style; place roll in lined baking pan.

☝ Line a baking pan with baking parchment. Put the cake rolls into the pan (no more than two rolls in one pan, so they can bake without sticking to each other).

☝ Brush the tops with beaten egg. If you wish, sprinkle sesame seeds over it. Prick with a fork to allow for even rising. Let the rolls stand in the pan for about 20 minutes before baking.

☝ Preheat the oven to 375°F (190°C). Bake for about 40 minutes until nicely browned.

Preparing the sweet buns: Prepare cake rolls with cocoa or cinnamon filling as described above. Slice each roll into 1-inch slices. Place cut side down in pan with about 1 inch between the buns so they can rise without sticking together. You can bake the buns as one large unit by placing the buns close to each other on the tray.

Preparing the nut crescents: With the nut filling, you can prepare cake rolls as described above or make delicate crescents. The crescents can be filled with the cocoa or cinnamon filling instead.

☞ On a floured surface, roll each packet of dough into a 10–12 inch circle. Cut each circle into 12 or 16 pie-shaped wedges, depending on the size crescent you want.

☞ In a bowl, stir nuts, candied orange peel or raisins, and sugar. You can add 1 teaspoon lemon rind, if you wish. Spread the wedges with honey or jam. (You can spread them on the circle of dough before cutting into wedges.) Sprinkle a small amount of filling over each wedge. Beginning at wide edge, roll toward point. Curve edges for crescent shape. Put the crescents in a lined baking pan, leaving ½ inch between them. Brush beaten egg over the tops. Let rise for 20 minutes.

☞ Bake at 350°F (180°C) for 25 minutes.

Preparing the cheese pockets: With the cheese filling, you can prepare cake rolls as described above or make cheese pockets.

☞ Combine cheese, sugar, egg yolks, vanilla, and raisins. Mix well.

☞ On a floured surface, roll each packet of dough into a square 6x6 inches. Cut into nine smaller squares, 2x2 inches each. Put one tablespoon filling in the middle of each square. Close each square by bringing the side points over the top, resembling an envelope. Press together well. We recommend using a toothpick to hold the edges together. (Remove it after baking.) Place on a lined baking pan, brush with beaten egg, and let rise for 20 minutes in the pan before baking.

☞ Bake in a 375°F (190°C) oven for about 25 minutes.

Marzipan ring: Mix the marzipan well with the egg whites. Put the mixture in a decorating tube.

☞ On a floured surface, roll a packet of dough into a long, narrow rectangle approximately 5x24 inches. Spread the marzipan, lengthwise, on the middle third of the sheet of dough. Fold into a roll by bringing the right-hand long side over the filling, then folding the left side over it. You will have a long, narrow roll. Make cuts in the top of the dough, 2 inches apart. Bring the ends together to form a circle, with the cuts on the outer side. Bake each ring on a separate pan.

☞ Brush the rings with egg yolks (mix with 2 tablespoons water, if you wish).

☞ Bake each ring in a preheated 375°F (190°C) oven for about 30 minutes.

☞ About 10 minutes before the cake ring finishes baking, sprinkle almond bits on the top.

☞ When the cake is finished baking, warm jam and drizzle it over the baked cake. Cool the cake on a rack. Serve uncut on a nice tray. Slice at the table.

YEAST CAKES

Sweet Buns, Crescents from Layered Yeast Dough, p. 215;
Rolled Yeast Cake, p. 220; Yeast Twist, p. 228

Rolled Yeast Cakes [picture on page 218]

The best yeast cake is the rolled cake. Possible fillings are numerous. Here we give you a cocoa filling and a cinnamon filling to choose from. These cakes freeze well.

DOUGH

Cold Yeast Dough, page 222

COCOA FILLING (FOR 2 CAKES)

¼ cup cocoa

1 cup sugar

3 tablespoons jam OR

   1 heaping tablespoon softened margarine

⅔ cups raisins — optional

1 tablespoon finely grated lemon rind

1 egg, beaten

handful sesame seeds — optional

CINNAMON FILLING (FOR 2 CAKES)

3 tablespoons jam

⅓ cup cinnamon

1½ cups sugar

1 cup chopped walnuts — optional

⅔ cup raisins — optional

Preparing the dough: Prepare one recipe of dough according to the instructions. Separate this dough into six balls. Each ball is sufficient for making one rolled cake.

Preparing the rolled cake: Roll a ball of dough into a rectangle, whose long side matches the length of the baking pan you will use. The sheet of dough should be about ¼-inch thick. Make the filling of your choice. Each filling recipe is enough for two cakes.

Preparing the cocoa cake: In a bowl, mix the cocoa and sugar. You can use this basic cocoa mixture, or add ingredients to suit your taste (for example, nuts). Spread the dough with the jam or softened margarine, and then sprinkle the cocoa mixture over the dough. If you wish to use raisins, sprinkle them over the cocoa mixture. Sprinkle lemon rind on top of all. Roll lengthwise, jelly-roll style.

Preparing the cinnamon cake: Spread jam on the dough. In a bowl, mix the cinnamon with the sugar. Sprinkle evenly over the dough. Sprinkle with nuts and/or raisins. Roll up in jelly-roll fashion.

Baking the cake: Line a pan with baking parchment. Put the cake (or two cakes) in the pan. Brush the top with beaten egg. If you choose, sprinkle sesame seeds over the egg. Prick the dough in several spots to allow for even rising and prevent the formation of air pockets.

Let the cake rise for about 20 minutes in the pan before baking.

Preheat the oven to 375°F (190°C). Bake for about 40 minutes, until nicely browned.

Variation: You can bake the cocoa- or cinnamon-filled cake rolls as individual buns by cutting each roll into 1-inch slices. Place cut side down in pan with about 1 inch between the buns so they can rise without sticking together. Alternatively, You can bake the buns as one large unit by placing the cut buns close to each other on the tray.

Bake at 350°F (180°C) for 25 minutes.

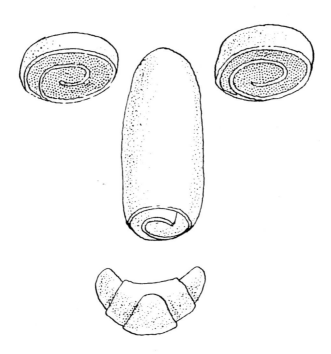

Cold Yeast Dough

A yeast dough that rises in the refrigerator and not at room temperature. The dough contains extra oil, and cakes made with it stay fresher longer. This dough freezes well.

10 cups flour
2 cups salted margarine, cubed and softened
1 cup sugar
1 level teaspoon salt
4 packages dry yeast or 4 ounces fresh
about 2 cups lukewarm water
5 eggs
2 tablespoons vanilla, OR
    finely grated lemon rind

☕ It is best to use the dough hook of an electric mixer for kneading.

☕ Sift the four into a bowl large enough to knead in it. Add the cubed margarine, sugar, and salt. Dissolve the yeast in a bowl with 1 cup lukewarm water (taken from the 2 cups), and add to the flour. Make sure the yeast does not touch the salt directly as that prevents the dough from rising. Add the remaining 1 cup water, eggs, and vanilla or lemon rind. Knead into an elastic dough.

☕ Lightly flour the top of the dough, and cover with a dishtowel. Place it in the refrigerator to rise for about 5 hours.

☕ Take the dough out of the refrigerator. Lightly flour a work surface. Grease and lightly flour 15x10-inch baking pans. If you prefer, you can line the pans with baking parchment.

☕ Shape the dough for baking as you wish. You can use the fillings given for other yeast recipes.

☕ The dough can easily be divided into six balls and used for six yeast cake rolls.

Rich Nut Rolls

A great yeast cake with a rich nut filling. You can make it nondairy or use dairy ingredients, if you prefer. The original filling uses hazelnuts, almonds, and candied orange peel. You can use nuts and raisins instead. Freezes well.

DOUGH (FOR 2 CAKE ROLLS)

6 cups flour

2 packages dry yeast

about 1⅓ cups lukewarm water (or milk)

½ cup salted margarine (or butter)

1 cup sugar

2 eggs

1 teaspoon grated lemon rind

FILLING

6 heaping tablespoons soft honey or jam

1 pound hazelnuts (can be part almonds, part hazelnuts)

8 ounces candied orange peel

1½ cups sugar

GLAZE

1 egg, beaten

Preparing the dough: Sift the flour into a large bowl. Dissolve the yeast in it. Add margarine, sugar, eggs, and lemon rind. Knead into a soft, pliable dough. Using an electric mixer with a dough hook makes the kneading easy. Put the dough in a bowl to rise. Flour it lightly, cover with a dishtowel, and let stand for an hour in a warm spot.

Preparing the loafs: Lightly flour a work surface. Grease or line with baking parchment a 15x10-inch pan. Divide the dough in two. Roll each part of the dough into a rectangle whose longer side is about 15 inches. Spread honey or jam on the sheet of dough.

In a bowl, stir the nuts, almonds, candied peel, and sugar until thoroughly combined. Sprinkle the mixture evenly over the two sheets of dough. Roll each sheet of dough up from the long side. Put the rolled dough, seam side down, into the baking pan. Let rise for another 10 minutes in the pan before baking. Brush the top with beaten egg.

Bake in a preheated 400°F (200°C) oven for 45 minutes until nicely browned. Turn off the oven. Let the pan stand for about 15 minutes in the oven before removing it.

"Golden Noodles" Cake

A wonderful, appealing yeast cake from the Hungarian kitchen made with simple ingredients. The cake consists of layered rounds of dough covered with sugar and nuts. Best when dairy, this delight can also be pareve. You bake this cake in a round pan, such as a tube pan, a Kugelhopf, or a springform pan. Freezes well.

DOUGH

4 cups flour

1 package dry yeast

1 cup lukewarm milk or water

⅓ cup sugar

2 egg yolks

3 teaspoons vanilla

pinch salt

½ teaspoon grated lemon rind

½ cup butter or margarine

FILLING

1 cup chopped nuts

¼ cup sugar

1 teaspoon cinnamon or lemon rind

¼ cup melted butter or margarine

Preparing the dough: Sift flour into a bowl. In a separate bowl dissolve the yeast in ½ cup of milk (or water) and 1 teaspoon sugar. Make a well in the flour, and pour in the yeast. Add the remaining liquid, sugar, egg yolks, vanilla, salt, lemon, and softened butter. Knead well into a soft dough that separates from the sides of the bowl. You may have to add a handful of flour as you work. Lightly flour the ball of dough, and cover it with a dishtowel. Let rise for 90 minutes, until doubled in size.

Assembling the cake: Grease a tube pan or fluted Kugelhopf pan or springform well. Mix the nuts, sugar, and cinnamon in a small bowl.

♗ Lightly flour a work surface. Roll the dough out until it is ¼-inch high. With a round cookie cutter or the edge of a drinking glass, cut rounds of dough. Dip each round in melted butter, and arrange them as the first layer in the baking pan. Sprinkle part of the nut mixture over them. Cover all with a second layer of butter-dipped rounds, and sprinkle part of the nut mixture over it. Repeat until all the dough and nut mixture has been used.

♗ Let rise for 20 minutes. Bake 45 minutes in a preheated 375°F (190°C) oven until the surface is lightly browned. The cake is best when fresh.

Kugelhopf

A wonderful yeast cake. This cake has no filling but is enriched with raisins, and you can add almonds, too. Freezes well.

DOUGH

1 package dry yeast

1½ cups lukewarm water or milk

5 cups flour

¾ cup salted margarine or butter

2 eggs

1 cup sugar

1 teaspoon vanilla

⅓ cup raisins

pinch salt

1 teaspoon grated lemon rind

1 cup chopped almonds

DECORATION

powdered sugar

♟ Dissolve the yeast in a glass with ½ cup lukewarm water (taken from the total). Let stand for a few minutes. Sift the flour into a large bowl. Form a well in the middle and pour the dissolved yeast into it. Add the remainder of the water, margarine, eggs, sugar, vanilla, raisins, salt, and lemon rind. Knead into a soft dough.

♟ Lightly flour a Kugelhopf pan. (It is the correct size when the dough only reaches halfway up the side of the pan — that leaves room for rising.) Sprinkle the chopped almonds on the bottom and sides of the pan. Line it with the dough, pressing it into an even layer. Sprinkle lightly with flour, cover with a dishtowel, and let rise for about 2½ hours.

♟ Bake in a preheated 375°F (190°C) oven for about 1 hour.

♟ Cool and turn out onto a serving tray.

♟ Before serving, sprinkle the cake with powdered sugar.

YEAST CAKES

Streusel Kuchen

A delicious Austrian cake. Its name comes from its streusel crumb topping. Best when eaten fresh from the oven. If you bake it in a rectangular pan, the servings will be to the height of the pan. If you would like to have tall, narrow slices, double the quantities (but not the amount of yeast) and bake it in a tube pan. You do not have to double the amount of crumbs. Either way, streusel cake is recommended for anyone who loves a tasty, satisfying pastry that has no filling or frosting. This cake freezes well.

DOUGH

2 cups flour

1 package dry yeast

3 tablespoons sugar

½ cup lukewarm water or milk

1 egg

¼ cup margarine or butter, at room temperature

½ lemon — juice and finely grated rind

½ teaspoon vanilla or flavoring

STREUSEL-CRUMB TOPPING

3½ cups flour

1 cup sugar

1 tablespoon grated lemon rind

1 teaspoon cinnamon

1¼ cups soft margarine or butter

Preparing the dough: Sift the flour. Use the "old-fashioned way" for the yeast dough; make a well in the flour, and put the yeast in it. Cover it with 1 tablespoon of the sugar and pour over it ½ the water (or milk) — mix it lightly with your fingers. Cover the bowl with a dishtowel, and let stand for 15 minutes until the yeast doubles in size.

Add the remaining sugar, water (or milk), and egg. Melt the margarine and add it. Add flavoring — lemon juice and rind, vanilla or rum flavoring. Knead the dough well, until it no longer clings to the side of the bowl. Cover with a dishtowel, and let rise for about 20 minutes until doubled in size.

Lightly flour a work surface. Roll the dough out to a 9x13-inch rectangle to fit the size of the baking pan. Grease the pan, and line it with the dough, pressing it into the corners. Let rise for another 15 minutes.

Preparing the crumbs: In a bowl, mix the flour, sugar, lemon rind, and cinnamon. Soften one cup margarine, add it to bowl, and continue to mix until crumbly.

Melt the remaining ¼ cup margarine. Brush some of it over the dough in the pan. Sprinkle the crumbs evenly on top. Then drizzle the remaining melted margarine over the crumbs.

Bake in a preheated 400°F (200°C) oven for about 20 minutes until the crumbs are nicely browned.

Cut into slices and serve fresh.

Yeast Twists [picture on page 218]

The best, most versatile yeast doughs can be baked in many variations. Here we are giving you a great basic recipe with an interesting result. You do not spread the filling on a sheet of dough and then roll it up in the usual way, but rather you make three strips filled with a cocoa cream and braid them. The amounts listed are sufficient for three twists that can be baked in one large pan. You can top it all with a lemon or vanilla glaze. These twists freeze well.

DOUGH

6 cups flour
2 packages dry yeast
about ¾ cup lukewarm water
½ cup sugar
1 cup salted margarine
¼ cup oil
3 eggs
pinch salt

FILLING

1 cup unsalted margarine, at room temperature, cubed
1¼ cups sugar
4 tablespoons cocoa
2 tablespoons liqueur or rum
4 teaspoons vanilla

GLAZE

⅓ cup water
¼ cup sugar
juice of half a lemon, OR
    1 tablespoon vanilla

Preparing the dough: Sift the flour into a bowl. Dissolve the yeast in the water, and add to the flour. Add remaining ingredients, and knead into a soft dough. Using an electric mixer with a dough hook makes the kneading easier. Lightly flour the ball of dough, cover with a dishtowel, and let rise for 1 hour in a warm place. The dough rises a bit but does not double in size.

☕ Lightly flour a work surface. Divide the dough into three parts for three twists. Work with one part at a time.

☕ Line a 15x10-inch pan with baking parchment.

Preparing the twists: Put the cubed margarine into the container of a food processor or blender. Add the other ingredients, and blend until you have a smooth, fine creamy filling. Divide the filling into nine portions, to match the number of strips you will make.

🍳 Divide the first portion of dough into three parts. Roll each of the three into a rectangle, with the long side the same length as that of the baking pan.

🍳 Spread each sheet of dough with a portion of the filling. Roll each rectangle, and seal its edge. Pinch together the edges of the three rolled strands and braid. Place the twist in the baking pan. Prepare two more twists with the other two portions of the dough. The three twists can be right next to each other in the pan.

🍳 Bake in a preheated 350°F (180°C) oven for 45 minutes until nicely browned.

Preparing the glaze: In a small bowl, beat the water, sugar, and lemon juice or vanilla. Drizzle the glaze over the baked twists.

🍳 Let the cakes remain in the oven, with the heat off, for another 10 minutes.

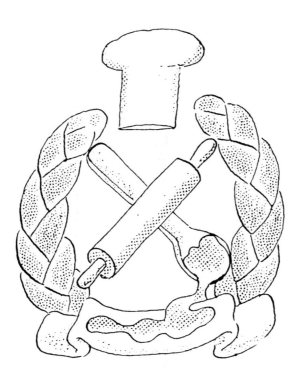

229

LAYERED CAKES add variety and flair to your baking. Some have a number of layers from the same type of batter — such as Fluden — and different types of fillings. Others have two layers of batter or dough with a frosted layer between them, such as Torte with Flaky Pastry. A layered cake can also have a cookie base, a pudding filling, and a whipped topping, as in the Cookie and Pudding Layer Cake. A devotee of baking can assemble layered cakes from recipes at hand, adding frostings, whipped toppings, and fruit layers that blend well together. The possibilities are endless. Layered cakes are often decorated. They are beautiful and are impressive to serve at *simchas*.

Layered Cakes

Rich Fluden

The Fluden is considered the most prestigious among the outstanding Hungarian baked goods. The dough is flaky and delicate, the filling very rich. The cake consists of four layers with various fillings — nuts, poppy seed, and apples. A dusting of powdered sugar tops it all. This cake is especially fitting for Purim and parties. The dough also serves for Hamentashen and crescents. This cake freezes well.

DOUGH

4 cups flour

1 ounce yeast

about ⅓ cup orange juice or water

4 egg yolks

2 cups salted margarine

4 tablespoons sugar

NUT FILLING

1½ cups walnuts, ground

⅔ cup sugar

rind of one lemon, finely grated

2 tablespoons jam

POPPY SEED FILLING

2 tablespoons jam, for spreading

3½ ounces ground poppy seed

⅔ cup sugar

⅓ cup sweet wine

1 generous tablespoon salted margarine

APPLE FILLING

5 tart apples

½ cup sugar

½ lemon — juice and finely grated rind

pinch of cinnamon

3 tablespoons cake or bread crumbs

TOPPING

1 egg yolk mixed with 1 tablespoon water

powdered sugar

Preparing the dough: Sift the flour into a bowl. Dissolve the yeast in the liquids. Add the yeast and the remaining ingredients to the flour. Knead into elastic dough, easy to work with. Shape the dough into a ball and refrigerate, covered, for two to three hours.

☞ Remove the dough from the refrigerator and place on a floured surface. Divide the dough into four equal portions.

☞ Lightly grease a 9x13-inch baking pan. Roll one portion of the dough to the size of the baking pan. Place it in the pan. (Roll it lightly around the rolling pin to move it.)

Preparing the nut filling: In a bowl, mix the ground nuts, sugar, and lemon.

☞ Spread the jam over the dough in the pan. Sprinkle the filling evenly over the jam. Roll out a second portion of the dough, and cover the nut filling with it.

Preparing the poppy seed filling: Spread the jam evenly over the second layer of dough. Put the poppy seed, sugar, wine, and margarine into a saucepan. Cook over medium heat while stirring with a wooden spoon until the margarine melts. Take care that the poppy seeds do not burn.

☞ Spread the poppy seed mixture evenly over the jam. Roll the third portion of dough, and place it over the poppy seed mixture.

Preparing the apple filling: Wash, dry, and core the apples. It is not necessary to peel them. Coarsely grate the apples into a bowl. Lightly squeeze out the extra juice and set aside. (It makes a wonderful drink.) Add the sugar, lemon, and cinnamon. Stir the mixture gently.

☞ Sprinkle the crumbs over the third layer of dough. Sprinkle the apple mixture over the crumbs. Roll the fourth portion of dough large enough to cover the edges of the pan. Cover the apple mixture with the dough.

☞ Score the top or prick well with a fork to let steam escape. Brush egg yolk over the dough.

☞ Bake in preheated 350°F (180°C) oven for 45 minutes until lightly browned.

☞ Before serving, dust the top of the cake with powdered sugar using a fine-meshed sifter.

LAYERED CAKES

Flecked Torte with Flaky Pastry

A rich, beautiful cake, fit for simchas. This light, tasty torte is flecked with grated chocolate. The torte comes between two layers of flaky crust and chocolate frosting. Powdered sugar dusts the top. From this large sheet cake you cut many portions. If you do not want such a high cake, decrease all ingredients by one-third. Treat the baked crusts gently as they have a tendency to break. Freezes well.

TORTE

8 eggs, separated

3 egg whites

2 cups sugar

¾ cup wine or juice

½ cup oil

4 ounces bittersweet chocolate, grated fine

2½ cups flour

4 teaspoons baking powder

FLAKY CRUST

⅓ cup sugar

1½ cups salted margarine

3 egg yolks

3 cups flour

3 teaspoons baking powder

about ⅓ cup water or juice

FROSTING

1 cup powdered sugar

1 cup unsalted margarine

2 eggs

1 tablespoon rum flavoring

3 tablespoons cocoa powder

1 tablespoon instant coffee

DECORATION

powdered sugar

Preparing the Torte: Put yolks in large bowl. Beat lightly with 1 cup sugar. Mix in wine, oil, and chocolate.

In a separate bowl, beat the egg whites until stiff, gradually adding the remaining sugar. Gently fold beaten whites into yolk mixture. Fold in flour.

Line a 15x10x2-inch baking pan with baking parchment, with edges of paper extending beyond edge of pan. Pour in cake batter.

Bake in preheated 350°F (180°C) oven for 50 minutes. Insert toothpick to see if cake is done. When toothpick comes out clean, the cake is ready. Remove cake from oven and put on table.

Preparing the crust: In a bowl, beat the sugar and margarine. Beat in the egg yolks. Mix in flour and baking powder with enough liquid to make a pliable, easy-to-roll dough.

Divide the dough into two parts. On a lightly floured work surface, roll each part into a rectangle slightly larger than the baking pan. (The dough will shrink a bit while baking.) Prick with fork to prevent air bubbles.

Lightly grease the outside of two baking pans the same size as the pan you used for the torte. Place the rolled dough on the outside of the pans.

Bake at 350°F (180°C) for 15 minutes until lightly browned.

Preparing the frosting: Put the powdered sugar into a blender or food processor. Add remaining ingredients. Blend until frosting is smooth and velvety. Refrigerate for 1 hour.

Assembling the cake: Put one of the crusts on a tray. Spread half of the frosting over it. Place flecked torte over frosting. Spread with other half of frosting. Cover with second crust. Sprinkle powdered sugar on top.

Refrigerate until served. Serve in thin slices.

LAYERED CAKES

Meringue and Whipped Cream Layered Cake

The very name of this cake tells you it is a great dessert. The base is a flaky crust covered with jam. Over that comes a layer of pudding and whipped topping. (You can make this cake dairy or pareve.) Above the pudding is a meringue on which you drizzle chocolate glaze. Each slice shows off the different toned layers. A cake that melts in your mouth. This cake freezes well.

DOUGH

2 cups self-rising flour

½ cup salted margarine, cubed

3 egg yolks

2 tablespoons sugar

½ teaspoon finely grated lemon rind

about ⅓ cup juice or water

2 tablespoons jam

WHIPPED LAYER

DAIRY

1 cup whipping cream

1 package instant vanilla pudding mix

1 cup cold milk

NONDAIRY

1 cup nondairy topping whip

1 package instant vanilla pudding mix

1 cup nondairy milk substitute

MERINGUE

4 egg whites

¾ cup sugar

CHOCOLATE GLAZE

2 tablespoons cocoa

½ cup sugar

3–4 tablespoons water

¼ cup unsalted margarine

A tip on making this cake: The easiest way to make this cake is to first bake the meringue, take it out of the pan, and set it aside. Then bake the flaky pastry, the base layer, in the same pan. Prepare the whipped filling and the glaze. Then assemble the cake.

Meringue layer: Put egg whites into a bowl. Beat until stiff peaks form, gradually adding sugar.

☞ Line a 9x13-inch baking pan with baking parchment. Spoon the egg white into the pan, and gently smooth the top with a spatula.

☞ Bake in a preheated 275°F (140°C) oven for about 1 hour until dry and delicately golden. Carefully remove the meringue from the pan by lifting it with the baking parchment. Place it on the table to cool.

Preparing the pastry: Sift flour into a bowl. Cut the cubed margarine into the flour until pieces are the size of small peas. Add egg yolks, sugar, and lemon rind. Continue to knead, adding just enough liquid to make a soft, pliable dough.

☞ Lightly flour the pan used for the meringue. Press dough evenly into the pan.

☞ Bake in a preheated 350°F (180°C) oven for about 20 minutes until lightly browned.

Preparing the whipped layer:

DAIRY: Put whipping cream, pudding mix, and milk into a bowl. Beat until thick.

NONDAIRY: Beat nondairy topping until foamy. Add the pudding mix and liquid, alternately. Continue to beat until firm.

Preparing the chocolate glaze: Put cocoa, sugar, and water into a small saucepan. Stir over medium heat until a syrup forms. Turn off heat and add margarine, stirring until it melts.

Assembling the cake: Spread jam evenly over the base pastry layer. Cover with whipped pudding. Use baking parchment to support the pudding. (After refrigeration, it will hold its own shape.) Carefully turn the baked meringue over the whipped layer. Peel off the baking parchment from the meringue. Drizzle chocolate glaze over the meringue. Freeze for 2–3 hours until firm. Then refrigerate until served.

Vanilla Filled Layered Cake

A wonderful, easy-to-make cake. Only the whipped top layer is baked. Every slice is reminiscent of a sandwich cookie with rich filling. This cake does not freeze well.

about ¾ pound plain cookies

FILLING

3½ cups water

1½ cups unsalted margarine, cubed

4 teaspoons vanilla

1¼ cups sugar

4 egg yolks, beaten

6 heaping tablespoons flour

1 lemon — juice and finely grated rind

TOPPING

4 egg whites

8 tablespoons sugar

½ cup flaked coconut — optional

☞ Line a 9x13-inch baking pan with half the cookies.

Preparing the filling: Pour water into a pot. Add cubed margarine, vanilla, sugar, beaten egg yolks, flour, and lemon. Mix well and bring to boil, stirring constantly. When mixture thickens into a pudding, pour over the cookies.

☞ Cover the pudding with another layer of cookies.

Preparing the topping: In a separate bowl, beat the egg whites until stiff, gradually adding sugar. Cover the cookies with the beaten egg whites. Smooth gently with a spatula. Sprinkle flaked coconut over top, if you wish.

☞ Bake in a preheated 350°F (180°C) oven for about 10 minutes, until lightly golden.

☞ Refrigerate until served.

Vanilla Mousse Layered Cake

An easy-to-make cake, delicious as well as impressive. This cake has three layers: a flaky base, a whipped layer and a chocolate crumb top. Freezes well.

DOUGH

3 cups flour

2 teaspoons baking powder

1 cup salted margarine

3 tablespoons sugar

5 egg yolks

about ⅓ cup juice or water

MOUSSE FILLING

5 egg whites

½ cup sugar

1 package instant vanilla pudding mix

about 2 tablespoons jam

TOPPING

dough crumbs

2 ounces bittersweet chocolate, coarsely grated

Preparing the dough: Sift flour and baking powder into bowl. Cut in margarine until pieces are size of small peas. Add sugar, yolks, and juice. The dough should be soft and pliable. Remove a fist-size piece of dough and put it in the freezer. This portion will be used for topping. Cover the remaining dough, and refrigerate for about 1 hour.

♟ Lightly flour a 9x11-inch baking pan. Press the dough into it evenly.

♟ Bake in a preheated 350°F (180°C) for 15 minutes; crust will be partially baked.

Preparing the mousse filling: Beat the egg whites until peaks are firm, gradually adding the sugar. Add the pudding mix, and continue to beat until mixture is smooth.

♟ Spread the baked crust with a thin layer of jam. Spoon the filling over it.

♟ Remove dough from freezer. Coarsely grate it over the mousse. Sprinkle the grated chocolate over all.

♟ Return pan to oven. Lower oven to 300°F (100°C). Continue to bake for another 40 minutes until delicately browned.

Elegant Poppy Seed Layer Cake

This delicious cake has a rich poppy seed filling on a base of flaky dough, and is topped with meringue. Perfect for Purim or any simcha. It freezes well.

DOUGH

2½ cups flour
2 teaspoons baking powder
1 cup salted margarine, cubed
2 egg yolks
⅓ cup sugar
finely grated rind of 1 lemon
about ⅓ cup juice or water

FILLING

1 cup salted margarine
1 cup sugar
5 egg yolks
3 cups ground poppy seed
½ cup sweet wine
1½ cups flour
pinch baking powder

MERINGUE

7 egg whites
1 cup sugar

Preparing the dough: Sift flour and baking powder into a bowl. Cut in margarine until pieces are size of small peas. Add yolks, sugar, lemon rind, and liquid. Knead and work into a soft, pliable dough. Press the dough into a lightly-floured, medium-sized baking pan.

Preparing the filling: Lightly cream margarine and sugar until smooth. Mix in egg yolks, poppy seed, and wine. Fold in flour and baking powder. Spread filling over the dough.

☞ Bake in a preheated 350°F (180°C) oven for 45 minutes.

Preparing the meringue: Beat egg whites until peaks are firm, gradually adding sugar.

☞ Remove cake from oven. Gently spread meringue evenly over filling.

☞ Lower oven to 300°F (100°C), and bake 15 minutes more until lightly browned.

Poppy Seed Filled Layers

A special, tasty cake with a poppy seed filling. Its layers are made from yeast dough. You can top with a chocolate glaze or powdered sugar. Freezes well.

DOUGH

5 cups flour

1 cake compressed yeast

about ¾ cup lukewarm water

2 cups salted margarine, cubed

4 tablespoons sugar

4 egg yolks

FILLING

4 tablespoons honey

3 cups ground poppy seed

2 tablespoons margarine

2 tablespoons jam

1 tablespoon cinnamon — optional

1 lemon — juice and finely grated rind

1 cup sugar

about 2 tablespoons wine or water

Preparing the dough: Sift flour into a bowl. Dissolve yeast in ½ cup lukewarm water (taken from total water) and add to flour. Add cubed margarine, sugar, and egg yolks. Combine well, and knead into a pliable dough. You may need to adjust the amount of water as you work. Lightly flour the ball of dough; cover with a dishtowel. Refrigerate for about 2 hours.

Preparing the first layer: Lightly flour a work surface. Line a 9x13-inch pan with baking parchment. Divide the ball of dough into three parts. Roll each part into a rectangle the size of the baking pan. Line the pan with the first rectangle of dough. Spread about 2 tablespoons of soft honey on it.

Preparing the filling: Put all ingredients except honey into a saucepan. Cook for five minutes over medium heat, stirring constantly with a wooden spoon. Spoon half of the mixture over the honey.

Assembling the cake: Place the second dough rectangle over the poppy seed filling. Spread the remaining honey over it, and spoon the remaining filling over the honey. Cover with the third dough rectangle. Prick well with fork to prevent air bubbles.

☞ Bake for 40 minutes in a preheated 350°F (180°C) oven until nicely browned.

Coffee Filled Layers

A tasty, attractive cake composed of three layers of cold yeast dough with a whipped coffee filling between them. This cake freezes well.

DOUGH

Poppy Seed Filled Layers yeast dough, page 241

FILLING

3 heaping tablespoons jam
4 egg whites
¾ cup sugar
1 heaping tablespoon instant coffee

DECORATION

powdered sugar

Preparing the dough: Follow recipe instructions for dough.

Preparing the cake: Lightly flour a work surface. Line a 9x13-inch baking pan with baking parchment or lightly grease the pan.

♧ Divide the ball of dough into three parts. Roll each part into a sheet the size of the baking pan. Line the pan with the first sheet, and spread half the jam on it.

Preparing the filling: Put the egg whites into a bowl. Gradually adding the sugar, beat the egg whites until stiff peaks form. Gently stir in the instant coffee.

Assembling the cake: Spread half of the beaten egg white over the jam. Place the second sheet over the egg white. Spread the remaining jam over it, and then spread the remainder of the egg white on top of that. Cover with the third sheet.

♧ Prick the top sheet with a fork many times to allow steam to escape while baking.

♧ Bake in a preheated 350°F (180°C) oven for about 40 minutes until lightly browned.

♧ Dust the cake with powdered sugar.

Whipped Cream and Crumb Cake

A light, delectable cake with a flaky base. The filling is made from dairy whipping cream or nondairy substitute. A crumb layer tops the cake. Freezes well.

DOUGH

2½ cups flour, sifted

1½ teaspoons baking powder

2 eggs

⅓ cup sugar

1 cup salted margarine, softened

COFFEE GLAZE — OPTIONAL

½ teaspoon instant coffee powder

1 teaspoon sugar

¾ cup water

FILLING

DAIRY

1 cup whipping cream

1 cup milk

1 package vanilla-flavor instant pudding mix

NONDAIRY

1 cup nondairy whipping cream

1 cup nondairy milk substitute

1 package *pareve* vanilla-flavor instant pudding mix

Preparing the dough: Put all ingredients into a bowl and knead into a dough. Lightly grease a 9x11-inch baking pan, and spread the dough in it. Bake in a preheated 350⁰ F (180⁰ C) oven 20 minutes until golden. Cool. Prepare crumbs by cutting off one-fifth of this layer and grating it coarsely.

Preparing the coffee glaze: Stir coffee powder and sugar in water. Drizzle over the baked dough.

Preparing the filling:
DAIRY: Pour whipping cream, milk, and instant pudding mix into a mixing bowl. Beat until the mixture is smooth.

NONDAIRY: Beat the nondairy whip until foamy. While beating, add the pudding mix and the liquid, alternately, and continue to whip until smooth and creamy.

Assembling the cake: Spread the cream over the baked layer. Sprinkle the crumbs evenly over the cream. Refrigerate until served.

Cream Filled Cake

A cake reminiscent of a children's favorite. The base is a thin, brown wafer. On top of it comes a layer of whipped pudding. Covering all is a layer of chocolate frosting. A light cake that melts in your mouth. Instead of the wafer base, you can use a chocolate cake. This cake freezes well.

DARK BASE

4 tablespoons cocoa powder

1 cup sugar

1 cup water

1 cup unsalted margarine, cut into cubes

8 egg yolks

1¾ cups flour

1½ teaspoons baking powder

WHIPPED PUDDING

8 egg whites

1 cup sugar

1 package instant vanilla pudding mix

CHOCOLATE FROSTING

4 tablespoons cocoa powder

7 tablespoons sugar

8 tablespoons water

4 ounces bittersweet chocolate, broken into squares — optional

1 tablespoon rum flavoring

1 cup unsalted margarine

Preparing the dark base: Put cocoa and sugar into a saucepan. Stir gently while adding water. Bring to boil over low heat. Remove from fire, and add margarine. Gently stir in the egg yolks. Continue to stir until margarine and yolks are thoroughly mixed in. Pour into a bowl. Fold in the flour and baking powder.

👨‍🍳 Lightly grease 9x13-inch baking pan. Spread batter evenly in the pan.

👨‍🍳 Bake in a preheated 350°F (180°C) oven for about 15 minutes (cake will be half-done).

Preparing the whipped pudding: Put egg whites into a mixing bowl. Beat with an electric mixer, gradually adding sugar and instant pudding mix. Continue to beat until the pudding is smooth.

♟ Remove baking pan from oven. With a spatula, spread the pudding evenly over cake layer.

♟ Return pan to oven, and continue to bake at 350°F (180°C) for another 15 minutes. After baking, the pudding layer is delicate and light colored.

Preparing the chocolate frosting: Put cocoa and sugar into a saucepan, and mix lightly. Add the water and squares of chocolate. Bring to boil over medium heat, stirring constantly to prevent burning. Continue to stir until syrup is smooth. Turn off heat. Stir in rum flavoring and cubed margarine. Continue to mix until the frosting is smooth.

♟ Gently pour the frosting over the pudding layer. Spread evenly with a spatula.

♟ Refrigerate the cake until served.

LAYERED CAKES

Chocolate Layered Cake

A tasty, pretty, easy to prepare cake. The base is flaky. The whipped, spiced filling is covered with crisp crumbs. This cake freezes well.

BASE

3 cups flour

4 teaspoons baking powder

1 cup salted margarine

⅓ cup sugar

2 teaspoons vanilla

5 egg yolks

about ⅓ cup juice or water

FILLING

4 ounces chocolate, coarsely grated

5 egg whites

1 cup sugar

3 tablespoons jam

3 heaping teaspoons cocoa powder

1 teaspoon instant coffee

1 teaspoon cinnamon

2–3 tablespoons boiling water

Preparing the base: Sift the flour and baking powder into a bowl. Cut the margarine into cubes, and add it to the flour. Begin to work it into crumbs. Stir in the sugar, vanilla, egg yolks, and juice or water. The dough must be smooth and soft — you may have to adjust the amount of liquid. Shape the dough into a ball.

Separate about one-third of the dough, and place it in the freezer. Line a lightly greased 15x10-inch baking pan with the remainder of the dough, pressing it with your fingers to create a uniform layer.

Preparing the filling: Sprinkle the grated chocolate over the dough. Beat the egg whites until firm, while gradually adding the sugar. In a separate bowl stir together the jam, cocoa, instant coffee, cinnamon, and water. Gently fold the combined ingredients into the beaten egg whites. Spread over the chocolate layer.

Remove the dough from the freezer, and grate it over the filling, trying to distribute the grated crumbs evenly.

Bake in a preheated 350°F (180°C) oven for 45 minutes until lightly browned.

Chocolate "Sandwich"

A delicious, pretty cake with a chocolate filling hiding between two layers of crisp pastry. This cake freezes well.

DOUGH

4 cups flour

3 egg yolks

1 cup salted margarine

4 teaspoons baking powder

4 tablespoons sugar

about ¾ cup orange juice or water

FILLING

2 cups sugar

2 tablespoons cocoa powder

½ cup water

½ cup unsalted margarine, cubed

8 ounces chocolate, broken into pieces

2 tablespoons flour

5 eggs

powdered sugar for dusting

Preparing the dough: Sift the flour into a bowl. Add the yolks, margarine, baking powder, sugar, and juice or water. Work the ingredients together into a pliable dough easy to roll out; shape into a ball. Divide the ball of dough into two equal parts. On top of baking parchment, roll one part of the dough to fit a 15x10-inch baking pan. Line the pan with the baking parchment and the rolled-out dough.

Preparing the filling: Put the sugar, cocoa, water, margarine, and chocolate into a saucepan. Cook over medium heat, stirring constantly until smooth and creamy. Cool the filling. Then stir in the flour and the eggs. *Another option:* You can separate the eggs, stir the yolks into the chocolate mixture, beat the whites until firm, and then fold them into the chocolate mixture. (You can also add the whites left over from the eggs used in the dough, and beat them with the other whites.)

☞ Spread the creamy filling over the sheet of dough. Roll the other part of the dough to just a bit larger than the baking pan. We recommend rolling this part, too, on baking parchment. Carefully turn this sheet of dough over the chocolate layer, and peel away the baking parchment. Prick the dough in many spots.

☞ Bake in a preheated 350°F (180°C) oven for 50 minutes until nicely golden.

☞ Sprinkle powdered sugar on top.

AS IN THE CAKE recipes, the cookies presented to you in this section are rich indeed. Baking cookies takes more time and work area than cake baking. Yet, after investing the effort, you have a lovely product that stores well. Children can help with the preparation of basic cookies in different shapes made with firm, tasty dough. Cookies can be enhanced with coconut, sesame seeds, almonds, or chocolate. Cookie doughs are versatile; they can be turned into various shapes, rolled and sliced, molded into round balls by hand, cut out with special cutters, or baked and cut into bars. Cookies add interest to the tray of baked goods with their wide range of varieties.

Cookies

Nut Strips

To make these tasty, attractive cookies, you bake a rich nut meringue base and when cool, slice into bars, and dip each end in chocolate. When finished, these cookies are spectacular, and add a special touch to simchas. They freeze well.

DOUGH

2½ cups self-rising flour

¾ cup unsalted margarine

5 egg yolks

⅔ cup ground walnuts

1½ cups powdered sugar

1 lemon — juice and grated rind

FILLING

2–3 tablespoons jam

5 egg whites

1 cup sugar

2 cups chopped nuts

2 tablespoons cocoa — optional

FROSTING

4 ounces bittersweet chocolate, broken into pieces

4 tablespoons water

¼ cup unsalted margarine

Preparing the dough: Sift flour into a bowl. Add margarine, cut into small cubes, and begin to work into the flour. While kneading, add the other ingredients. The dough will be soft and pliable.

♙ Grease a 9x13-inch baking pan, and line it with the dough, pressing it evenly.

♙ Bake at 350°F (180°C) for about 10 minutes until top is lightly golden. Remove from oven. Spread top with jam.

Preparing the filling: Beat egg whites until peaks are firm, gradually adding sugar. Fold in nuts and cocoa. Spread the mixture on top of the jam. Return the cake to the oven, and continue to bake at 350°F (180°C) for about 45 minutes.

Preparing the cookies: Cool the cake. Cut into rectangular strips, ¾ inch x 2½ inches. Place chocolate in a pan with water and margarine. Stir over a medium flame until melted evenly. Dip the two ends of each cookie into the heated chocolate, and put on a tray or baking rack to dry. Keep the cookies in the refrigerator.

Diamond Nut Cookies

You can use walnuts, almonds, or peanuts in these cookies. These crispy, tasty treats are sliced into medium-thick diamond shapes. They freeze well.

4 cups flour
4 teaspoons baking powder
1 cup sugar
¾ cup oil
1 cup salted margarine
2 eggs
1 teaspoon grated lemon rind
1 teaspoon cinnamon
1 teaspoon vanilla extract
2 cups ground walnuts

♟ Place all ingredients into a bowl and combine into a uniform dough

♟ Lightly grease a 9x13-inch baking pan. Spread the dough evenly in the pan. Cut the dough through with intersecting diagonal lines spaced about 1¼ inches apart.

♟ Bake at 350°F (180°C) until lightly browned, about 45 minutes.

♟ Cool, then gently separate the individual cookies. Store in a tightly closed container.

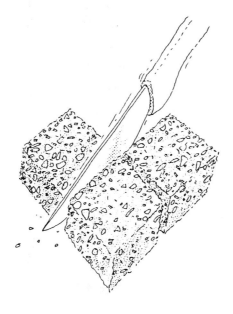

Nut Meringue Cookies

Tasty, rich, easy to prepare cookies. You make a crisp crust and cover it with a layer of nut meringue. These cookies freeze well.

 2½ cups self-rising flour
 1 cup salted margarine
 2 cups sugar
 1 teaspoon vanilla
 3 eggs, separated
 3 tablespoons jam
 ¾ cup walnuts, ground fine

♧ Sift flour into a bowl. Add margarine, cut into cubes, and begin to work it into the flour. Add 1 cup sugar, vanilla, and yolks. Combine the ingredients into a soft, pliable dough. If the dough is too dry, add a small amount of water or juice.

♧ Lightly grease a 9x13-inch baking pan. Place dough in pan in an even layer.

♧ Bake in a preheated 350°F (180°C) for about 15 minutes, until golden.

♧ Remove pan from oven and spread jam over the top. While gradually adding the remaining sugar, beat egg whites until the peaks hold their shape. Fold beaten whites into the ground nuts.

♧ Spread the nut mixture over the jam. Return the pan to the oven, and bake for about another 12 minutes until top is lightly browned.

♧ Remove pan from oven, cool slightly, then cut the cookies into rectangles.

Egg Cookies (Eier Kichel)

These are piquant, salty egg cookies, made with a generous amount of black pepper, that go well with herring and other savory foods. They are baked from a soft dough in very well-greased pans. When these cookies are ready, they are quite dry. Customarily, they are baked for Purim. These cookies freeze well.

    about 4 cups flour
    10 tablets artificial sweetener
    3 tablespoons cognac
    5 eggs
    scant ½ teaspoon black pepper
    pinch salt
    10 tablespoons oil
    additional oil for baking

♕ Sift flour into a bowl. In a glass, dissolve sweetener in cognac. Add cognac mixture, eggs, pepper, and salt to the flour. Combine all the ingredients into a soft dough that sticks to your hands.

♕ Generously flour a work surface. Divide dough into three equal parts. Roll each part into a rectangle about ¼-inch thick. Cut dough into asymmetrical rectangular shapes of various sizes. Score top of each cookie with a fork to a depth of $\frac{1}{16}$ of an inch (each cookie should be about 2¼ inches by 3½ inches).

♕ Pour oil to a depth of about 1 inch into a large baking pan. (If necessary, use additional baking pans.) Arrange the cookies in the pan; they will expand while baking. Place the pan on the upper rack in your oven.

♕ Bake the cookies in a preheated 350°F (180°C) oven for about 20 minutes until they are lightly browned. Turn the cookies over, and continue to bake until done.

♕ Store the cookies in a closed container.

Crescent Cookies

Crispy, thin, scrumptious cookies. These cookies freeze well.

8 cups flour
6 teaspoons baking powder
2½ cups salted margarine, cubed
½ cup sugar
2 teaspoons vanilla
2 eggs
½ cup water

COATING

powdered sugar

🍫 Sift flour and baking powder into a bowl. Add cubed margarine, and begin to work into a dough. Add the remaining ingredients, and knead until you have a smooth, elastic dough ready for rolling. Shape into a ball, and refrigerate for 30 minutes.

🍫 Line a large baking pan with baking parchment. Lightly flour a work surface. Divide chilled dough into two parts. Shape each part into a roll 1½ inches in diameter. Cut into thin slices, and shape into a crescent.

🍫 Bake in a preheated 350°F (180°C) oven for 10–15 minutes until nicely golden.

🍫 Put powdered sugar in a saucer, and roll the baked cookies in it while still warm.

🍫 Store the cookies in a closed container.

Sugar Cookies

The best cookies are usually the simple, traditional ones. These crispy cookies can be enriched with coconut, sesame, cinnamon, walnuts, or chocolate. These cookies freeze well.

12 cups flour
6 teaspoons baking powder
1 cup salted margarine
6.5 fluid ounces oil
2½ cups sugar
6 eggs
1 cup orange juice
finely grated rind of 1 lemon

VARIATIONS
2 cups sesame seeds, OR
2 cups coconut, OR
1–2 tablespoons cinnamon, OR
1 cup chopped walnuts, OR
3½ oz finely grated chocolate

♟ Put flour, baking powder, margarine, oil, sugar, eggs, juice, and lemon rind into the bowl of an electric mixer. Beat at medium speed until you have a soft, elastic dough ready for rolling. Add any of the ingredients for variation, if you wish.

♟ You will have to use a number of cookie sheets, as the amount of cookies produced by this recipe is quite large. Line each sheet with baking parchment.

You can make the cookies in a number of ways:

1) Roll the dough to a thickness of ¼-inch, and cut out round or shaped cookies.

2) Use a cookie press; choose the blade for long, thick cookies.

3) Shape round walnut-size pieces of dough, and place them on the cookie sheet.

♟ After shaping the cookies, place them close to each other on cookie sheets.

♟ Bake at 350°F (180°C). The flat cookies will be nicely golden in about 10 minutes. The pressed and the round cookies take a few minutes longer.

♟ Cool and store in a closed container.

COOKIES

Eggless Sugar Cookies

Crispy, tasty, light cookies. Their uniqueness is that they are made without eggs. They can be made even more dietetic if you use an artificial sweetener in place of the sugar. These cookies freeze well.

8 cups flour
1½ cups orange juice or water
1½ cups oil
1½ cups sesame seeds or coconut
1½ cups sugar
pinch salt
6 teaspoons baking powder

♔ Sift the flour into a bowl. While kneading, add water, oil, sesame or coconut, sugar, salt, and baking powder. Knead into a uniform dough.

♔ Lightly flour a work surface. Divide the dough into four balls. Knead and roll each ball into a rectangle ⅛-inch thick.

♔ You can cut out circles of dough using the edge of a drinking glass; you can cut squares with a pastry wheel, or make different shapes with a knife.

♔ Line large cookie trays with baking parchment. Place the cookies close to each other on the tray.

♔ Bake in a preheated 375°F (190°C) oven for about 20 minutes until nicely golden.

♔ Cool the cookies, and store in a closed container.

Chocolate Nut Cookies

Rich, exquisite cookies covered with chocolate and bits of nuts. The cookies are cut into squares after baking. They freeze well.

  2½ cups self-rising flour
  1 cup salted margarine, cubed
  1 cup sugar
  1 teaspoon vanilla
  1 egg
  5 ounces bittersweet chocolate
  1 cup chopped nuts

☙ Sift flour into a bowl. Add margarine, sugar, vanilla, and egg. Combine into a soft, pliable dough.

☙ Lightly grease a 9x13-inch baking pan, and spread dough evenly in it.

☙ Bake in a preheated 350° F (180° C) oven until lightly browned, about 20 minutes. Remove pan from the oven.

☙ Melt chocolate in top of a double boiler over boiling water. Spread melted chocolate over baked base. Distribute nuts evenly over the chocolate. Cut into squares.

No-Bake Cheese Balls

Delicacies can also be made with little effort. These cheese cookies are made with cream cheese, crumbs, and flavorings. They can be rolled in coconut, chocolate shot, or ground nuts. Cheese balls freeze well.

½ cup sugar
¼ cup soft margarine or butter
8 ounces cream cheese
1 tablespoon grated lemon rind
6 tablespoons raisins
1 teaspoon vanilla
2 cups cookie or cake crumbs

♕ Cream sugar and margarine. Add cheese, lemon rind, raisins, vanilla, and crumbs. Mix until dough is thoroughly blended.

♕ With moistened hands form, plum-sized cheese balls. Roll each ball in the ingredient of your choice: coconut, chocolate shot, or ground nuts. Place each ball in a cupcake paper. Refrigerate until served.

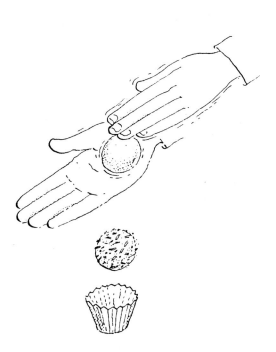

Savory Cheese Cookies

Thin cheese cookies with a salty taste. They're easy to make, quick to bake, and yield large batches. These cookies freeze well.

1 pound cream cheese
4 ounces salty white cheese
½ teaspoon salt — optional
2 ounces grated yellow cheese
2 cups salted margarine
5 cups flour

TOPPING
1 egg, beaten
2 ounces sesame seeds

☙ Put cheeses in a bowl and mix. Beat the flour and margarine in well. Taste and adjust the seasonings, if necessary. Shape the dough into a ball.

☙ Refrigerate the dough for one hour.

☙ Lightly flour a work surface. Divide the dough into four parts. Roll each part into a large, thin sheet, about ⅛-inch thick. Cut out rounds of dough.

☙ Line cookie trays with baking parchment. Place the cookies on the tray close to each other. Brush with beaten egg, and sprinkle with sesame seeds.

☙ Preheat oven to 400°F (200°C), and bake each tray for 20 minutes until cookies are lightly browned. While baking, the cookies puff up and then shrink. Their texture is similar to puff pastry, and they are tastiest when freshly baked.

COOKIES

Wonderful Honey Cookies

Flat, tasty cookies, easy to prepare. They can be made richer by topping with chopped almonds. These cookies freeze well.

½ cup sugar
3 eggs
4 tablespoons honey
pinch cinnamon
pinch cloves
1 level teaspoon baking soda
½ cup salted margarine
4 cups flour

TOPPING — OPTIONAL
1 egg, beaten
1 cup chopped almonds

♧ Place all the ingredients into a bowl in the order listed. Knead into a soft dough.

♧ Lightly flour a work surface. Roll the dough into a large sheet ¼-inch thick. Cut into small rounds. Place the cookies on baking sheets lined with baking parchment.

♧ You can brush the cookie tops with beaten egg, and sprinkle with chopped almonds.

♧ Bake in a preheated 375°F (190°C) oven for 20 minutes until lightly browned. When the cookies are ready, they are still soft. They become firm after standing a few minutes at room temperature.

♧ When the cookies have cooled, store them in a well-sealed container.

Hungarian Honey Cookies

Delicate cookies easy to prepare — and a particularly large batch. These cookies freeze well.

   1 cup honey
   2 cups sugar
   6 eggs
   1½ cups salted margarine
   1 teaspoon cinnamon
   1 teaspoon ground cloves
   1 teaspoon instant coffee
   1 teaspoon baking soda
   8–10 cups flour

♟ Put all ingredients into a bowl. Combine and knead into a soft dough, easy to roll out. You may have to adjust the amount of flour; add as necessary.

♟ Liberally flour a work surface. Keep some sifted flour available in case you need it when rolling the dough. Break off a handful of dough, and roll it to a thickness of about ⅓ inch. Cut out circles of dough using a small drinking glass. Gather the scraps of dough, and roll them out again.

♟ Line large cookie trays with baking parchment, and place cookies on them, leaving space between them — they spread while baking.

♟ Bake at 375°F (190°C) for 25–30 minutes until nicely browned.

♟ Let cookies cool. Store in a closed container.

COOKIES

Honey Cookies

Wonderful, dark and crispy, these cookies freeze well.

6 level tablespoons honey
1½ cups sugar
⅔ cup oil
4 eggs
1 level teaspoon ground cloves
1 level teaspoon cinnamon
1 level teaspoon instant coffee
1 level teaspoon baking soda
about 6 cups flour

Put honey, sugar, oil, eggs, and spice into a bowl. Stir with a wooden spoon. Add flour. The dough will be soft and sticky. You may have to add more flour.

Line a large cookie tray with baking parchment. With floured fingers, pull off pieces of dough about the size of a small plum, and shape into a ball. Place the balls of dough on the tray, leaving space between them. Flatten each dough ball.

Bake at 375°F (190°C) for about 20 minutes until browned. The cookies become firm as they cool and take on an arched shape.

The cookies keep well in a closed container.

Glazed Honey Cookies

Wonderful honey cookies, each topped with a frothy, shiny white crown. It is easy to make a large batch of these especially tasty cookies. These cookies freeze well.

3½ cups flour
1 teaspoon baking powder
¼ cup sugar
pinch salt
1 egg
1 egg yolk
¾ cup oil
¾ cup honey
3 tablespoons sesame seeds — optional
1 teaspoon cinnamon
1 level teaspoon ground cloves
1 tablespoon lemon rind, finely grated

TOPPING
1 egg white
1 cup powdered sugar
2 tablespoons lemon juice

☞ Sift flour and baking powder into a bowl. Add all other ingredients, and mix or knead into a soft, uniform dough.

☞ Line two large cookie trays with baking parchment.

☞ Pull off walnut-size pieces of dough, and shape into round cookies. Place them on the cookie tray, about 1 inch apart. Flatten the balls of dough.

☞ Bake at 350°F (180°C) for about 25 minutes. The cookies become firm after baking.

Preparing the glaze: Beat the egg white to a shiny firmness, gradually adding the sugar. Add lemon juice and mix gently. Spread egg white mixture over the cookies while they are still warm. Let the cookies dry at room temperature for about an hour.

☞ Store the shiny honey cookies in a closed container to keep them crispy.

Chocolate Balls [picture on page 270]

Wonderful, round cookies rich with chocolate frosting. Another special feature of these cookies is that they are a great way to use leftover cake or cookies. You can serve cookies in paper holders, add a chocolate glaze, and top them with a candied cherry, a walnut, or coconut flakes. Freezes well.

½ cup cocoa

1 tablespoon instant coffee

1 cup sugar

2 tablespoons liqueur, wine, or rum flavoring

½ cup boiling water

½ cup unsalted margarine, cubed

12 ounces cookies or leftover cake

½ cup raisins or chopped nuts — optional

DECORATION — OPTIONAL

chocolate frosting

coconut flakes

candied cherries

walnut halves

Preparing the frosting: Put cocoa, instant coffee, sugar, liqueur, and water into a saucepan. Stir over medium heat until the ingredients combine into a syrup. Remove from heat, and add cubed margarine. Mix well until frosting is smooth.

Preparing the cookies: Crumble the cookies or leftover cake. Pour the chocolate syrup over the crumbs, and stir the mixture well until it is uniform. You can make the cookies richer with walnuts and raisins.

👨‍🍳 With moistened hands, make balls of dough about the size of a plum. The balls can be even more special by dipping into chocolate syrup and then into coconut flakes.

👨‍🍳 Arrange the chocolate balls in paper cookie holders. If the balls have been dipped only in chocolate, you can put a candied cherry or walnut half in their center.

👨‍🍳 Refrigerate the chocolate balls until serving.

Variation: Chocolate "sausage" — Have ready baking parchment or aluminum foil. Shape the cookie dough into a roll, 2 inches in diameter. Wrap and freeze until firm. Cut thin slices of the chocolate sausage, and serve on a plate.

Sephardic Cookies [picture on page 270]

Light yet filling cookies, these sesame-covered rings originated among the Spanish Jews, where they were called biscochos. These cookies freeze well.

8 cups flour
1 ounce yeast
about 1½ cups lukewarm water
1 teaspoon sugar
¾ cup oil
½ teaspoon black pepper
1 tablespoon salt
1 cup salted margarine

TOPPING
1 egg, beaten
sesame seeds, OR
    coarse salt

☞ Sift flour into a large bowl. Dissolve yeast in ½ cup water (from the total amount listed) and sugar. Let stand for a few minutes. Make a well in the flour, and pour in dissolved yeast, oil, and seasonings. Add margarine, and begin to combine the ingredients into a dough. Gradually add remaining water while kneading — as needed.

☞ Lightly grease a large baking pan, or line it with baking parchment. Make finger-thick strips of dough 6 inches long. Shape each strip into a circle by pressing the ends together. Put the cookies in the pan, leaving a small amount of space between each. If you prefer, you can bake the dough strips as straight cookies, without turning them into rounds.

☞ Spread beaten egg over each cookie. Sprinkle sesame seeds or coarse salt on top.

☞ Bake at 400°F (200°C) for about 25 minutes until lightly browned.

☞ Cool and store in a closed container.

COOKIES

Meringue Cookies

Luscious, tasty, light cookies — a flaky pastry and a meringue top. You can make them richer with bits of nuts, chocolate sprinkles, and so on. These cookies freeze well.

1¾ cups self-rising flour
1 cup salted margarine, at room temperature
1 cup sugar
2 tablespoons vanilla
2 eggs, separated

♟ Sift flour into a bowl. Add softened margarine, ½ cup sugar, vanilla, and egg yolks. Mix into a pliable dough, easy to roll out. Shape dough into a ball, wrap, and refrigerate for 30 minutes.

♟ Liberally flour a work surface. Roll the dough to a sheet ¼-inch thick. Cut out rounds with a cookie cutter or edge of a drinking glass. Put the cookies on cookie sheets lined with baking parchment.

♟ Beat egg whites until stiff, gradually adding remaining sugar. Spread ½ level teaspoon over each cookie.

♟ Bake in a preheated 375°F (190°C) oven for about 25 minutes.

♟ Cool and store in a tightly closed container.

Variation: You can top the meringue with bits of nuts, chocolate sprinkles, or colored sprinkles by following the instructions below.

♟ Bake the cookies for 15 minutes *without* the beaten egg whites. Then spread the meringue over the cookies, add any topping you want, and return the cookies to the oven to bake until done. This way the toppings will maintain their colors.

Caraway Sticks

Tasty, salty sticks, baked from yeast dough and covered with caraway seeds. These freeze well.

4 cups flour
1 ounce yeast
½ cup lukewarm water
pinch sugar
½ cup salted margarine, at room temperature
¾ cup sour cream, OR
    about ¾ cup water
½ teaspoon salt

TOPPING
1 egg, beaten
handful of caraway or sesame seeds

♟ Sift flour into a bowl; make a well in the middle. Dissolve yeast in lukewarm water, and pour it into the well. Add sugar, softened margarine, liquids, and salt. Knead into a soft dough. Shape into a ball, and let dough rest for 30 minutes.

♟ Divide ball of dough into rolls, 1½ inches in diameter. Cut thin, narrow pieces from the rolls, and shape into strips about 2½ inches long and ½ thick.

♟ Put the strips on cookie sheets. Brush with beaten egg, and sprinkle with caraway seed or sesame seed.

♟ Bake in a preheated 375°F (190°C) oven for about 25 minutes until nicely browned.

♟ Cool and store in a tightly closed container.

Granola Cookies

Cookies rich in nature's bounty. The round, speckled cookies are rich in nuts, bran, sesame seeds, and coconut. You can also add raisins and even chocolate sprinkles. These cookies freeze well.

    2 cups self-rising flour
    2 cups bran
    1 cup sugar
    ½ cup salted margarine
    ½ cup coconut flakes
    ½ cup chopped walnuts or almonds
    ½ cup sesame seeds
    2 eggs
    1 orange — juice and finely grated rind
    1 teaspoon lemon rind
    1 tablespoon vanilla

Sift flour into a bowl. Stir in all other ingredients. Knead into a soft dough. Line two large cookie sheets with baking parchment.

Moisten your hands, and break off plum-sized pieces of dough. Put the pieces of dough on the trays, and flatten them a bit. Leave some space between cookies.

Bake in a preheated 400°F (200°C) oven for about 30 minutes.

Cool the cookies, and store in a closed container.

Toast Cookies [picture on page 270]

Leftover challah and breads can be toasted and put to use as crumbs. By adding other ingredients and kneading it all, you can produce tasty, crispy cookies. These cookies freeze well.

1 ½ cups finely crushed toast crumbs

2 cups flour

3 teaspoons baking powder

2 eggs

1 cup sugar

¾ cup salted margarine

juice of 1 lemon or orange

1 teaspoon vanilla extract

1 teaspoon vanilla or almond flavoring

2 tablespoons cocoa — optional

TOPPING — OPTIONAL

½ cup sesame seeds, OR

½ cup ground walnuts

☙ Put the toast crumbs into a bowl large enough for kneading. Add flour and baking powder. While adding the other ingredients, knead into a flexible dough. For brown cookies, add cocoa powder.

☙ Line a cookie sheet with baking parchment.

☙ Pinch off plum-sized pieces of dough, and put them on the sheet, flattening the ends a bit. You can sprinkle the tops with sesame seeds or ground nuts.

☙ Bake at 350°F (180°C) for 20 minutes.

☙ Cool and store in a tightly sealed container.

Flaky Pastry Pockets

Delicate cookies folded over to cover jam filling. With powdered sugar on their tops, these cookies are attractive on a serving plate. These cookies freeze well.

2½ cups flour
¾ cup sugar
1 teaspoon vanilla extract
1 teaspoon grated lemon rind
¾ cup butter and margarine
2 eggs, separated

FILLING

1 cup thick jam

DECORATION

powdered sugar

♧ Sift flour into a bowl. Stir in sugar, vanilla, lemon, margarine, 1 yolk, and egg. Knead into a pliable dough, easy to roll. You may need additional flour to make dough easier to work with. Shape into a ball, cover, and refrigerate for 30 minutes.

♧ Liberally flour a work surface — the dough tends to stick. Divide the ball of dough into two parts. Roll each part to a thickness of about ⅛-inch.

♧ Cut into 3-inch rounds, preferably using a cutter with a serrated edge. (Dough is sufficient for about 40 cookies.) Put ½ teaspoon jam in center of each round. Spread edge of round with egg white. Fold each round in half, and press to seal edges firmly.

♧ Put the cookies on cookie sheets lined with baking parchment.

♧ Bake at 400°F (200°C) for 12–15 minutes until golden brown.

♧ Cool the cookies. Sprinkle with powdered sugar before serving.

♧ Store in a closed container.

Mandelbread

These are hard, crisp cookies studded with chopped almonds or chocolate chips. You first bake rolls of dough, slice them, and return them to the oven until toasted. In Jerusalem these are called "kamish cookies"; the almond version is mandelbread. It is a good idea to make a double batch of these cookies — one almond and the other chocolate. These cookies freeze well.

COOKIE BASE

3 cups flour

3 teaspoons baking powder

1 ⅓ cups sugar

3 eggs

4 tablespoons oil

¼ cup salted margarine

FLAVORINGS

ALMOND COOKIES

4 ounces almonds, coarsely chopped

rind of 1 lemon, finely grated

CHOCOLATE COOKIES

½ cup chocolate chips

1 tablespoon vanilla

1 egg, beaten, with 1-2 tablespoons of water, as needed

☕ Sift flour and baking powder into a bowl. Add the other ingredients, depending on which flavor cookie you want. Mix well into a soft dough.

☕ With floured hands, shape two rolls, each about 12 inches long and 1½ inches in diameter. Brush beaten egg on the rolls. Put the rolls on an oven tray or cookie sheet which has been covered with baking parchment. You can bake all four rolls on one tray.

☕ Bake at 400°F (200°C) for about 45 minutes.

☕ Remove rolls from tray, and cut into slices about ½-inch thick. Lay each piece, cut side down, on cookie tray. Return cookies to oven, and let them toast on all sides until golden brown.

☕ The cookies store well in a closed container.

Oatmeal Cookies

Crisp, crunchy cookies studded with nuts and raisins. These cookies freeze well.

¾ cup margarine
1 heaping cup sugar
1 egg
¼ cup water
1 teaspoon vanilla extract
1 teaspoon salt
1 teaspoon cinnamon
½ teaspoon baking soda
1 cup raisins
1 cup walnuts, coarsely chopped
1 cup flour
3½ cups rolled oats

Put all ingredients into a bowl in the order listed, and mix into a dough. The dough is a bit soft and sticky.

Line a cookie tray with baking parchment. With moistened hands, break off plum-size pieces of dough and roll them into balls. Put on the tray, 2 inches apart. They swell during baking, then flatten out.

Bake in a 350°F (180°C) oven for about 25 minutes until dry. Remove from tray to cool on rack — they become crispier.

Store in a tightly closed container.

Sesame Squares

Very tasty, easy-to-make cookies. Mix the dough, and bake it as a single sheet. When the baking is finished, cut the cookies into squares. That's it! These cookies freeze well.

1¼ cups flour
1½ teaspoons baking powder
1 pound sesame seeds
1¼ cups sugar
½ cup oil
2 eggs

☙ Sift the flour into a bowl. Add the remaining ingredients, and mix well. Lightly grease two 9x13-inch baking pans. Divide the dough into two, and spread each part into a baking pan.

☙ Bake in a preheated 400°F (200°C) for 30 minutes.

☙ Remove from oven, and cut immediately into squares about 1¼ inches x 1¼ inches.

☙ When cookies are cool and firm, remove them from the pan and store in a tightly closed container.

Sesame Rounds

Tasty cookies, crisp and easy to prepare. You bake them as four rolls and slice into pieces after baking. These cookies freeze well.

2½ cups self-rising flour
1 cup salted margarine
1 cup sugar
2 teaspoons vanilla
1 cup sesame seeds
2 eggs

🍳 Sift flour into a bowl. Add all other ingredients, and mix into a soft, uniform dough.

🍳 Line a 9x13-inch baking pan with baking parchment. Divide dough into four equal parts, and shape dough into rolls about 1½ inches in diameter and the length of the pan. Place in the pan.

🍳 Bake in a preheated 375°F (190°C) oven for about 30 minutes until nicely golden.

🍳 Cut warm roll into thin slices. Cool and store in a tightly closed container.

🍳 To increase crispiness, you can place the cut cookies in a single layer on a cookie sheet and bake another 10 minutes.

Sesame Cookies [picture on page 270]

A crispy taste-treat. These cookies are easy to make, and batches are large. You cut the dough into circles with the edge of a drinking glass; change sizes by using different size glasses. These cookies freeze well.

4 cups flour

3 teaspoons baking powder

1 cup oil

8 ounces sesame seeds

finely grated rind of 1 medium lemon

2 eggs

1 cup sugar

about ½ cup orange juice or water

☞ Sift flour and baking powder into a bowl. Add other ingredients. Work into a pliable dough easy to roll out. You may have to adjust the amount of liquids.

☞ Lightly flour a work surface. Roll dough to a thickness of about ⅛-inch. Cut out rounds with edge of medium-size drinking glass. Shape dough remnants into a ball. Roll out again, and cut into rounds.

☞ Grease a large cookie tray, or line it with baking parchment. Place cookies on tray, leaving small amount of space between each.

☞ Bake in a preheated 375°F (190°C) oven for about 20 minutes until golden.

☞ Cool, remove from tray, and store in closed container.

COOKIES

Chocolate Pretzels

These brown, crispy pretzel-shaped cookies can also be baked as rounds. These cookies freeze well.

    1 cup salted margarine
    1½ cups sugar
    1 egg
    1 teaspoon vanilla extract
    2 heaping tablespoons cocoa
    3 cups flour

♟ Put all ingredients into a bowl in the order listed. Mix and knead into a soft, pliable ball of dough.

♟ Line a cookie tray with baking parchment.

♟ Divide the dough into about 50 pieces. Shape each piece into a strip about 6 inches long. Form a figure-8 with each strip of dough; pinch the ends together and place on prepared tray. (Instead of making pretzel shapes, you can break off pieces of dough and shape them into small balls. Place on cookie tray, and press a hole in the centers with your finger.)

♟ Bake in a preheated 350°F (180°C) oven for about 25 minutes.

♟ The cookies are dark brown and become crisp as they cool. When cool, store in a tightly sealed container.

Chocolate Chip Cookies

If you are out of chocolate chips, you can use coarsely grated chocolate. These cookies freeze well.

1 cup salted margarine
1½ cups sugar
2 eggs
2 teaspoons vanilla extract
1½ cups chocolate chips
about 2½ cups flour
½ teaspoon baking soda

☙ Mix all ingredients, except the chocolate chips, into a soft dough. Add chocolate chips.

☙ Lightly flour a work surface. Roll dough to a thickness of ⅛-inch. Cut out rounds with a drinking glass. Place cookies on baking parchment-lined cookie trays.

☙ Bake at 375°F (190°C) for 10–12 minutes.

☙ The cookies become crispy as they cool. When cool, store in a tightly closed container.

Chocolate and Orange Cookies

Crisp, tasty cookies. The chocolate mixture is made even richer by adding juice and rind of an orange. These cookies freeze well.

½ cup salted margarine
1½ cups sugar
1 egg
1 orange — juice and grated rind
2 tablespoons chocolate liqueur
4 ounces chocolate chips
1 teaspoon vanilla
1 cup chopped almonds — optional
about 3 cups flour
2½ teaspoons baking powder

♕ Mix and knead all ingredients into a soft mixture.

♕ Moisten your fingers, and make two rolls of dough with a diameter of 1½ to 2 inches. Wrap each roll in tin foil, and freeze for a few hours. Cut rolls into very thin slices. Put cookies on large cookie trays — the cookies spread while baking.

♕ Bake in a preheated 350°F (190°C) oven for about 25 minutes.

♕ Cool. The cookies harden after baking.

♕ Store in a closed container.

Almond Cookies [picture on page 270]

Crispy, delicate, delectable cookies. You can cut out flat, round cookies with a drinking glass or shape them into balls. These cookies freeze well.

2 cups flour
1¼ cups salted margarine, at room temperature
¾ cup sugar
1 cup chopped almonds
1 egg
pinch salt

DECORATION
powdered sugar

♟ Sift flour into a bowl. Add margarine, sugar, almonds, egg, and salt. Stir and knead into a soft dough. Shape into a ball.

♟ Line two cookie sheets with baking parchment. Pinch off pieces of dough and shape them into small balls, or roll out the dough to a thickness of ⅛-inch and cut out rounds using a drinking glass. Place the cookies on the tray.

♟ Bake in a preheated 350°F (180°C) oven for about 20 minutes until golden.

♟ Remove from oven. While still warm, dust with powdered sugar. Cool.

♟ Store in a closed container.

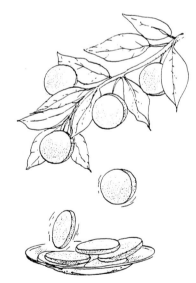

Potato Cookies

Crisp, light savory cookies made with mashed potatoes. Thesy are delicate and tasty — and offer you a way to use leftovers. These cookies freeze well.

1½ cups self-rising flour
1 cup mashed potatoes
1 cup salted margarine, at room temperature
1 egg
½ teaspoon salt

COATING
1 egg, beaten
handful of sesame seeds OR
    ½ cup fried onions — optional

☙ Sift flour into a bowl. Add mashed potatoes, soft margarine, egg, and salt. Mix well, and knead into a soft dough ready for rolling. If necessary, add a small amount of flour as you work.

☙ Roll dough into a rectangle about ⅛-inch thick. Cut out cookies with the edge of a glass. Grease two cookie trays, and put the cookies on them.

☙ Brush with beaten egg. If you wish, sprinkle cookies with sesame seeds or fried onions.

☙ Bake at 375°F (190°C) for about 20 minutes until lightly browned.

☙ Remove from oven and cool. The cookies are best when fresh.

☙ Store in a closed container.

COOKIES

FROM A SIP on Shabbos to a toast in honor of a *simcha*, liqueurs are a standard part of Jewish celebrations. With little effort and only a small expense, you can make liqueurs of superior quality. The basic ingredient of home liqueurs is 95% alcohol. Alternatively, you can use 90 proof vodka (45% alcohol). For the best results, use the finest vodka. Some liqueurs require a short spin in a blender and are sweet and thick. Others are clear, and require seeds or fruits that have been soaked for several days. These liqueurs can be stored at room temperature, but the bottles must be tightly sealed. The aromas of all the liqueurs can be improved by adding alcohol according to your individual taste.

Home-made liqueurs make wonderful gifts for *mishlo'ach manos* and *simchas*. *Le-chayim!*

Liqueurs

Egg Liqueur

A full-bodied, clear liqueur with a delicate, special taste. It must be refrigerated because of the egg content. If too thick, dilute with a small amount of water.

    4 eggs
    1 cup sugar
    2 teaspoons pure vanilla extract
    1 cup 95% alcohol
    1 cup water

♕ Put all ingredients into a blender. Mix for two minutes until you have a smooth, thoroughly mixed liquid.

♕ Pour the liqueur into a bottle and seal tightly. Refrigerate until served.

Variation: In place of the alcohol, use 1⅓ cups vodka and reduce the amount of water to ⅓ cup.

Chocolate Liqueur

A thick, sweet liqueur loved by everyone. It must be refrigerated because of the egg content.

    1 pound sugar
    5 tablespoons cocoa powder
    1 tablespoon instant coffee powder
    1¾ cups water
    1 cup 95% alcohol
    2 eggs

♕ Put sugar, cocoa, coffee, and water into a saucepan, and bring to boil. Let mixture cool. Pour into a blender. Add the alcohol and the eggs, and blend well. Taste and adjust according to the amount of alcohol you would like and the thickness of the liqueur.

♕ Pour the liqueur into a bottle, and refrigerate until served.

Variation: In place of the alcohol, use 2 cups vodka and reduce the amount of water to ½ cup.

Esrog Liqueur

After Sukkos is over, you can continue to make use of your esrog for a drink you can make a blessing over on Shabbos and holidays. The clear, bright liqueur has a sharp taste. It can be stored with your other liquors.

2 yellow *esrog*s
1½ cups 95% alcohol
1 cup water
¾ cup sugar

♙ Wash and peel the *esrog*s. Put into a container, and cover with alcohol. Close the container tightly, and let it stand for two weeks to absorb the flavor.

♙ Pour the water and sugar into a saucepan, and bring to boil. Continue to cook until the sugar dissolves. Cool the syrup, and pour it into the alcohol container. Remove the *esrog*s, pour the liqueur into a bottle, and seal tightly.

Variation: In place of the alcohol, use 2⅓ cups vodka and reduce the amount of water to ⅓ cup.

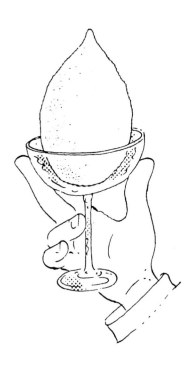

Coffee Liqueur

An excellent, clear liqueur with coffee flavor predominating. You can keep it in your bar; it stores well.

4 ounces high-quality Turkish coffee
5½ cups water
1⅓ cups sugar
1 tablespoon vanilla extract
1 tablespoon rum flavoring
2 cups 95% alcohol

☕ Place the coffee and 4 cups of water in a pan. Bring to a boil, and turn off the stove. Let the solution cool and the coffee grinds settle to the bottom.

☕ In a different pan, put the sugar and the remaining ½ cup water. Bring to a boil. Lower the flame, and continue to cook until the sugar dissolves.

☕ Being careful not to stir up the grinds, pour the clear coffee liquid — not the grinds — into the sugar syrup. Add the alcohol and flavoring, and stir well.

☕ Pour the liqueur into bottles, and seal well.

Variation: In place of the alcohol, use 3½ cups vodka and reduce the amount of water to 2⅓ cups.

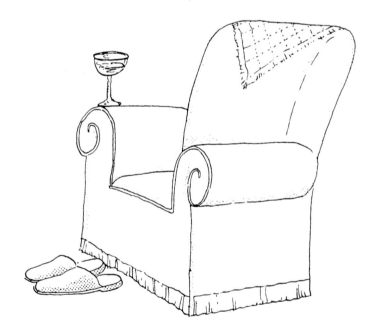

Caraway Liqueur

A special-tasting liqueur with the aroma of caraway and anise. It is a clear liquid with a light-green sheen. There is no need to refrigerate. You can buy the seeds in health food stores.

1 tablespoon caraway seeds
1 tablespoon anise seeds
1¼ cups 95% alcohol
1 cup sugar
1¼ cups water

♟ Put caraway and anise seeds in a jar. Pour alcohol over them, and seal jar well. Let the mixture absorb the flavors for five days in the kitchen pantry.

♟ Set aside about ¼ cup of the water. Pour remaining water into a saucepan, and add the sugar. Bring to a boil, and continue to cook over a low flame until sugar dissolves. Let cool.

♟ Strain the seeds from the alcohol solution, and set them aside. Pour the alcohol into the sugar syrup. Put the strained seeds into a small saucepan, and pour the reserved ¼ cup of water over them. Bring the water with the seeds to a boil, and then pour it all into the liqueur.

♟ Pour the liqueur into bottles, and seal tightly.

Variation: In place of the alcohol, use 2 cups vodka and reduce the amount of water to ⅔ cups.

Cherry Liqueur

A simple way to make cherry liqueur that does not require preserving the fruit for a long period, but rather making do with short-term soaking of the cherries. The liqueur you make tastes wonderful and has a lovely color. You can store this liqueur in your liquor cabinet.

2 pounds fresh cherries
2⅔ cups 95% alcohol
2 cups water
2 cups sugar

Remove the stems from the cherries, and pit them. Put the cherries into a jar, and cover them with alcohol. Close the jar tightly, and let it stand for five days.

Pour the water into a saucepan, and add the sugar. Bring the combination to a boil. Continue to cook over a low flame until the sugar dissolves. Cool. Add the cooled sugar syrup to the alcohol with the cherries, and stir well. Taste and adjust, if necessary.

Pour the liqueur with the fruit into bottles, and seal tightly.

Variation: In place of the alcohol, use 4 cups vodka and reduce the amount of water to 6.5 fluid ounces.

Lemon Liqueur

A sharp, easy-to-prepare liqueur with a clear, delicate tone. This liqueur can be kept with your other liquors.

> 2 large, ripe lemons
> 3 cups (one 650 ml bottle) 95% alcohol
> 3 cups water
> 2 cups sugar

☞ Peel the lemon and put the peel in a container. Pour the alcohol over the lemons and seal the container tightly. Let the lemons in the alcohol stand for a week to absorb the flavor.

☞ After the alcohol has absorbed the lemon flavor, pour the water into a saucepan and add the sugar. Bring to a boil, and continue to cook over a low flame until the sugar dissolves.

☞ Cool the sugar syrup. Remove the lemons, and pour the syrup into the alcohol. Shake well, taste, and adjust the flavor, if necessary. Pour the liqueur into bottles, and seal well.

Variation: In place of the alcohol, use 4 cups vodka and reduce the amount of water to 6.5 fluid ounces.

Cherry Brandy

A sweet, thick cherry brandy made from wine and alcohol. You can use a medium-quality wine and dried cherries, and the results will be attractive and a treat to drink. This brandy can be stored with your other liquors.

2⅔ cups sweet red wine
1 cup sugar
½ cup dried cherries
scant cup of 95% alcohol

☕ Pour the wine into a container, and add the sugar. Stir in the cherries, and seal the container well. Let the flavors mingle for about a month.

☕ After the flavors have been absorbed, pour the alcohol into the mixture and stir. Taste and adjust, if necessary, to the desired strength.

☕ Pour the brandy, with the fruit, into bottles and close tightly.

Variation: In place of the alcohol, use 2 cups vodka and reduce the amount of sweet red wine to 2 cups.

Index

INDEX

INDEX

Honey Cookies 262
Hungarian Honey Cookies 261
Mixer Honey Cake 64
Mock Honey Cake 66
Nougat Dobos 77
Nut and Poppy Seed Kindel 24
Peach Cake 177
Poppy Seed Filled Layers 241
Puzhon Crescents 136
Rich Honey Cake 65
Rich Nut Rolls 223
Vanilla Dobos 74
Wonderful Honey Cookies 260
Wonderful Honey Sponge Cake 62

K

Kindel 24
Kugelhopf 225

L

Layer cakes, see also Dobos cakes
Cheese Layer Cake 32
Chocolate Layered Cake 246
Chocolate "Sandwich" 247
Classic Apple Layer Cake 202
Coffee Filled Layers 242
Cream Filled Cake 244
Elegant Poppy Seed Layer Cake 240
Festive 3-Layer Sponge Cake 116
Flecked Torte with Flaky Pastry 234
Layered Apple Cake 208
Layered Cheesecake in Puff Pastry 34
Layered Cheese Festival 50
Layered Cheese Torte 52
Layered Coconut Cake 197
Layered Filled Sponge Cake 92
Layered Nut and Mousse Cake 14
Layered Yeast Dough 214
Layered Yeast Dough Cakes 215
Meringue and Whipped Cream
    Layered Cake 236
Poppy Seed Filled Layers 241

Puff Pastry Layered Nut Torte 10
Rich Fluden 232
Vanilla Filled Layered Cake 238
Vanilla Mousse Layered Cake 239
Whipped Cream & Crumb Cake 243
Wonderful Nut Cake Layers 26

Lemon
Lemon Cake 190
Lemon Liqueur 291
Lemon Meringue Pie 191
Nut Slices 18

Liqueurs
Caraway Liqueur 289
Cherry Brandy 292
Cherry Liqueur 290
Chocolate Liqueur 287
Coffee Liqueur 288
Egg Liqueur 286
Esrog Liqueur 286
Lemon Liqueur 291
Liqueur Sponge Cake 87

M

Mousse
Layered Nut and Mousse Cake 14
Nut and Mousse Cake 4

N

Nut
Almond-Base Torte 16
Apple Cake Roll 127
Apple Strudel 152
Baklava 148
Beautiful Spiral Torte 88
Carrot Cake I 185
Challah Torte 86
Chocolate Balls 264
Chocolate Nut Cookies 257
Dairy Nut Crescents 132
Diamond Nut Cookies 251
Dried-Fruit Cake 211

INDEX